COME AS YOU ARE:
CENTERING THE SELF IN FIRST-YEAR WRITING

Edited by
Alysa Robin Hantgan and Robert Mundy

Copyright © 2025 Pace University Press
All rights reserved. No part of this book may be reproduced,
stored in a retrieval system, or transmitted in any form, or by
any means, electronic, mechanical, photocopying, recording,
or otherwise, without prior permission of the publisher.

All unattributed chapters written by the editors Alysa Robin Hantgan and Robert Mundy

Artwork on pages 26, 28, 35, 38, 44, 96, 105, and 125 courtesy of Jenn Martins

Published by Pace University Press
41 Park Row
New York, NY 10038

PUPText, an imprint of Pace University Press

ISBN: 978-1-935625-89-6

Printed in the United States of America

COME AS YOU ARE: CENTERING THE SELF IN FIRST-YEAR WRITING

Acknowledgments — v

Introduction

"The Worst Crime is Faking It": A Practice of Writing the Self into the Academy — 1
Robert Mundy

Section One: Writing Foundations

1. Mapping the Academic Terrain Between High School and College Writing — 14
Justine Matias

2. Entering Academic Discourse Communities — 21
Jack N. Morales

3. Forging a Writing Process — 33
Christina Gonzalez

4. Toward an Understanding of Writing and Rhetoric — 37
Katherine Dye

5. Guided by Genre — 47
Genevieve Mills

6. Giving Credit Where Credit is Due — 55
Erika J. Pichardo

7. Engaging Writers in a Dialogue of Revision — 62
Zac Ginsburg

8. Writing Across the University — 71
Alicia Clark-Barnes

Section Two: Writing Projects

9. Course Introduction: Writing and Assessment — 80

10. Language and Identity — 85

11. Literacy Narrative — 88
Dana Jaye Cadman

12. Literacy Narrative Project — 93

13. Understanding Sources Through Genre Analysis   102
Jessica Kiebler

14. Genre Analysis Project   108

15. Writing An Opinion Editorial   120
Shirli Sela-Levavi

16. Opinion Editorial Project   123

17. Closing Reflection   131

Section Three: Student Voices

18. Centering the Student Writer   134
Alicia Clark-Barnes and Zac Ginsburg

19. Literacy Narrative   137
Gia Garofalo

20. Genre Analysis   139
Payton Cocchia

21. Student Sample: Opinion Editorials   141
George Provel
Victoria DiCecco

Editor and Contributor Bios   146

References   148

Acknowledgments

Come As You Are is the result of a commitment made by staff, faculty, and administration to writing studies and affordable instruction design. The result is a custom first-year writing text of tailored content that speaks with precision to Pace, Pleasantville's scaffolded core writing curriculum. In crafting *Come As You Are*, we have broken with traditional texts that are both expensive and unfocused, a costly one-size-fits-all design that forgoes local content and pedagogy to appeal to a general audience. *Come As You Are* is a move away from commercial education to programmatic intimacy, as students hear the voices of Pace instructors who, with each word on the page, help to develop and define the writing community found on our quaint Hudson Valley campus.

We would like to first recognize Associate Dean Bette Kirschstein, as this project would not have even been a consideration without her encouragement. Through her mentorship, we have evolved into a writing program of distinction. *Come As You Are* is the result of our colleagues who contributed their expertise to the collection. Often teaching several classes at multiple schools and/or taking on work commitments far beyond expectations, their willingness to embark on a project that required a generous offering of limited time is dedication personified. We are so deeply thankful to work with this incredibly gifted group of writers, poets, and academics. Maureen Colgan anchors the Department of English, Writing, and Cultural Studies. It is only because of her meticulous oversight of departmental needs that we could dedicate ourselves to this project.

We are also grateful to our partners outside of the writing program who have once again shown us that Pace's strength lies in its relationships and the support they provide. We offer our sincerest thanks to Dr. Joseph Franco, Dr. Sue Maxam, and Dr. Jim Stenerson, who initially advocated for high-quality and low-cost learning materials. The multi-year commitment to and financial support of open-educational resources made by the provost's office supported several open-access iterations that would eventually evolve into *Come As You Are*. We would also like to express our appreciation to Dean Tresmaine Grimes, Associate Dean Richard Schlesinger, and Dr. Nira Herrmann for providing research releases. Finding that money, however, is never an easy task, though Jane Ciampi, Arlene Bocskocsky, Erica Gonell, Rosa Lechuga, and Cristina Sullivan never left a stone unturned, resulting in summer workshops that greatly informed the text's purpose, subject matter, and organization.

The Mortola Library staff have been with us each step of the way. We are indebted to Sarah Burns Feyl and Jessica Kiebler, as their input and support have been instrumental in the building of our shared program. We are also grateful to Greg Murphy, Noreen McGuire, David Almodovar, Beth Gordon, and Tony Soares for their ongoing and long-standing commitment to affordable learning materials. Their collective support provided momentum for this project. We would like to extend a heartfelt thank you to Manuela Soares at Pace University Press, whose knowledge and expertise were and remain invaluable. When the inevitable personal and professional obstacles slowed down this process, her guidance helped us to regain our footing and move forward. *Come As You Are* would still be sitting on a shared doc in our Google Drive if not for Manuela. Thank you to Eileen Kreit, Vidhi Sampat, and the team at Pace University Press for skillfully, artfully, and efficiently taking our shared doc through a timely production cycle, ensuring we greet our students with print copies in time for the start of the semester.

We would not have been able to complete this project without finding additional time beyond our teaching and university commitments. Such an undertaking requires hours alone locked away from the world in our offices. When deadlines loom, time with loved ones is lost. Thank you to our families for encouraging us to carry on and complete this important project. Robert thanks his partner Rachel for her endless affection and tireless patience and daughter Ava Grace for reminding him that work is only a small part of his life. Alysa thanks her children, Emma, Sara, and Matthew, for their understanding, inspiration, and love.

At the end of the day, this is about our students–whose efforts deserve a cohesive and well-scaffolded course book rather than a loosely strung together selection of open-access texts. While *Come as You Are* is a programmatic milestone, we have already begun scribbling the early outline of our next book to ensure we continue to provide high-quality learning materials for all our core writing students. The only question that remains for now is which 90s artist will serve to guide its message.

INTRODUCTION

"THE WORST CRIME IS FAKING IT"[1]: A PRACTICE OF WRITING THE SELF INTO THE ACADEMY

Robert Mundy

HOW AND WHY WE WRITE

Welcome to ENG 110: Composition, the first of two offered first-year writing courses (FYW)[2] at Pace University. FYW is housed in the Department of English, Writing, and Cultural Studies and comprises courses that are part of a larger network of writing community and support, including writing in the disciplines (WID)[3], the Writing Center,[4] and Writing-Enhanced Course[5] program. FYW, as well as ENG 201 (WID), is a requirement of the Core Curriculum[6] and has been positioned as such, here at Pace University and across the country, in response to field-related scholarship and classroom experiences that have made abundantly clear the relationship between writing and academic success—not only in the writing classroom but across majors and disciplines. In the past, students may have associated writing with ELA, English, or Literature; however, at Pace University, all students across each major focus on writing since it is essential to success in the vast majority of careers and graduate programs that require the ability to locate, analyze, and synthesize information. Writing, therefore, is both field-specific and transferable, meaning that while each discipline has distinct writing expectations they also share similar conventions.

Beyond scoring a high grade or securing a well-paying job, writing also serves more intimate purposes, as the language we use, rhetoric we employ, and stories we tell form and reflect aspects of who we are, the characteristics of our unique identities. To write is to create and imagine–to explore and express emotion. To write is to feel, hurt, and heal–to be overcome by joy--to be fully human. Just as our words shape who we are, they are also shaped by our social and cultural environments. Writing, therefore, influences how we understand ourselves in relation to the world around us. It is a tool that builds communities and fosters a sense of connection. Its power can unite people around common goals that forge shared identities. Writing allows us to enter into public discourse, of which we participate perhaps more today than ever before. In the past, people consumed information

---

1 Kurt Cobain quote in Spin Magazine. "Nirvana: The 1994 Cover Story on Kurt Cobain's Death, 'Into the Black'"
2 Foundational course(s) offered by the majority of colleges and universities that introduces students to academic writing.
3 Course that teaches writing expectations and conventions associated with specific academic and professional fields.
4 Service that offers students support with writing in all academic disciplines at any stage of the writing process.
5 Integration of writing pedagogy into classes across academic disciplines. Chapter 8: "Writing Across the University" by Alicia Clark-Barnes explains the importance of writing across disciplines and majors.
6 Required undergraduate courses in the Liberal Arts and Sciences.

in the form of advertising, news, film, and television without a great ability to formally respond, whereas contemporary media, from the blogs we script and read, to social media posts we review and write, to the podcasts we create and listen, engage us and ask that we formulate a position. I say all of this not as a sales pitch, some attempt at making students writing converts, if they were not already. Rather, I am speaking about writing as *possibility*, particularly when entering a new academic experience.

LOCATING THE SELF IN ACADEMIC DISCOURSE

As curriculum creators and instructors of ENG 110 and contributors to this collection, we invite you to *come as you are* to first-year writing, as the book's title states, a phrase of which many readers may not be familiar since my references grow evermore dated with each new cohort that enters the university. Written by Kurt Cobain, Generation X's reclusive rock hero turned tragic figure, and recorded by his band Nirvana in 1991, the song "Come as You Are" first appeared on alternative radio 34 years ago, when grunge rock changed the music and cultural landscape, what seems like yesterday to me but is likely a relic of the last century for many–a silkscreened band t-shirt found on clearance racks at local Targets. Following its opening guitar riff, a haunting arrangement that feels as if each note is constrained and muted, somehow dampened by or played underwater, Cobain (1991) makes a contradictory request in his first verse to "Come as you are, / as you were / As I want you to be." If the first two lines signal acceptance for the present and past, the third, "as I want you to be," introduces a directive, eliciting feelings of tension and expectation.

Writing classes can feel similar, with teachers asking for authenticity, experience, and personal voice in one breath and then expecting prose that meets academic expectations and predetermined standards in the next, to be raw and polished at once, to come as you *are* and *were*, while at the same time take on an unfamiliar writing persona, the one you *should* be. Often, the result is a compromise of sorts in which students, aware of what is at stake, make an unspoken pact to give up some part of themselves and their history in order to become college writers. In some ways, this is the position of influential scholar David Bartholomae's (2005) widely read and commonly cited "Inventing the University,"--writing that values academic proficiency over personal voice: "...[students] have to invent the university by assembling and *mimicking* [emphasis added] its language...or they must dare to speak it, or to carry off the *bluff* [emphasis added]..." (Bartholomae, 1986, p. 5). He continued: "learning...becomes more a matter of *imitation* [emphasis added] or *parody* [emphasis added] than a matter of invention and discovery" (Bartholomae, 1986, p. 10-11).

I am of two minds when considering what Bartholomae proposed: Students must absolutely come to understand and navigate writing as a social act based on field-specific genres[7] and writing conventions, evidenced by our programmatic design that centers discourse communities as sites of inquiry across three courses[8]. However, and perhaps more importantly, the act of mimicking troubles me, as it is a hollow gesture that places the personal (private) and the academic (public) in opposition to one another, a binary that disparages the former and awards greater value to the latter. Furthermore, writing to

---

7 Chapter 5. "Guided by Genre" by Genevieve Mills provides a full review of this topic.
8 See section below titled "The Self and the Social" for further discussion of discourse communities.

invent and *discover* feels extremely necessary since it affords students time and space to explore new ideas, uncover new shapes in which to pour that thinking, and try on/out new voices and styles of writing. In short, I agree with Janine Rider (1990), who believed that educators, cannot "force [students] to adopt the language of the institution before they have anything to say" (p. 179).

In some ways, I align with Peter Elbow, a professor/scholar known for emphasizing personal expression, self-discovery, and the development of a writer's authentic voice. During the 1990s, he carried on a collegial debate with Bartholomae on the topic of authorship, a position Elbow believed students come to the university holding, whereas Bartholomae saw it as a marker of identity that needs to be attained. Elbow (1995) wrote:

> I invite [students] to write as though they are the central speaker at the center of the universe–rather than feeling, as they often do, that they must summarize what others have said and only make modest rejoinders from the edge of the conversation to all of the smart thoughts that have already been written. (p. 80)

Like Elbow, we ask our students to *come as they are* not as they have been *told* to be, to drop the pretense, avoid the posturing they have been taught, and engage with their professors and peers, along with themselves, openly, honestly, and genuinely. We say this in response to an educational system that has informed many students throughout primary and secondary school (and, sadly, in many higher education classrooms as well) that they are not welcomed in the very texts they are asked to produce, that to *sound* or *be* "academic" means to remove the self from their thoughts and words. Rodrigo Joseph Rodríguez's (2017)9 chapter in the provocatively titled collection *Bad Ideas About Writing* argued that at all times, "the writer needs to be present and breathing on the print or digital page" (p. 131).

WRITING INAUTHENTICITY

In previous writing classrooms, we suspect the use of the first person pronoun "I" was deemed unacceptable, without any explanation as to why or any discussion about genre and its attendant expectations. This silence results in students not trusting their voices or experiences, feeling detached from their assignments, and drafting prose that is unnatural and spurious. I am concerned with teaching practices that remove the writer from their own writing, leaving students to feel at odds with language, stuck between the dichotomy of colloquial (common)and academic (specialized), to effectively communicate or simulate sophistication. Asking students to bypass the self on their way to producing academic texts, we find ourselves promoting performance, a counterintuitive and counterproductive fake it till you make it scenario that isolates writing from the writer, meaning from experience, and thought from execution, all of which seem to be overlooked by Bartholomae (1986):

> To speak with authority student writers have not only to speak in another's voice but through another's "code"; and they not only have to do this, they

---

9 Chapter title: "Leave Yourself Out of Your Writing"

have to speak in the voice and through the codes of those of us with power and wisdom... (Bartholomae, 2005, p. 17)

Endless times, I have been told that "imitation is the sincerest form of flattery" but tend to agree with a latter adaptation of modified sentiment: "imitation is the homage mediocrity pays to superiority." Adulation places students in a passive position of obedience instead of offering a freedom to actively, creatively, and critically investigate writing and communication (hooks, 1994). Wisdom is not to be recapitulated–that's simply by no means how knowledge works. Instead, as celebrated philosopher and educator Paulo Freire (2000) argued nearly 60 years ago, "Knowledge emerges only through invention and re-invention, through the restless, impatient, continuing, hopeful inquiry human beings pursue in the world, with the world, and with each other" (p. 52).

I ask, as Rider (1990) has: must imitation be the mother of invention? When writing is framed as deference, many students must decouple language from understanding to adopt an intimidating, if not wholly inauthentic new language that must resonate on its own authoritative merits. As such, students frequently write to impress, stringing together endless thoughts in an attempt to seem knowledgeable and searching the digital thesaurus for polysyllabic synonyms to replace perfectly acceptable monosyllabic words. They have been told to never "write like they speak," as *good writing* needs to be complex, nearly impenetrable, a secret of sorts that the reader is left to grapple with and possibly decode, if they are lucky.

Lee A. Tonouchi (2004) does a wonderful job displaying what this attempt at sounding *academic* all too often looks like on the page: When I ascertain questions from my friend in pertainment to college, I try to replies with my own experience which will help adapt the college background to her. College for me will help because when I give my cooperation to others, especially kids, I can resolve a problem that is able enough to solve and to be able to 'win-win' on both parties in the end (p. 76).

As Tonouchi attested, students are applauded and praised when they conjure up dense prose, even when what is said makes little sense. His students' reactions to the above excerpt make this clear: "How bad-ass is [the writer]?" (p. 76). In such scenarios, attempts at prematurely engaging an academic register undermine the writer from forming an original, individual position and communicating that thinking—what is or should be their priority. Instead, student writing is a disembodied, cognitively detached act where the action takes place outside of the person in some undisclosed parallel space. This is the result of the separation between the self and the text that was mentioned above, a form or sense of erasure that leads students to treat knowledge as if it exists outside of who they are, information that is always just out of reach and only attainable through direct instruction or what Freire (2000) called the "banking model"--where the teacher deposits information into passive listeners, a form of rote learning and memorization that renders students anxious, dependent, and indistinguishable from one another. Prescriptive writing instruction is an overbearing approach to teaching and learning that seeks to codify communication–what in many ways, is an innate act. Imagine attempting to assign steps to something as natural as, say, breathing–the person would hyperventilate, possibly even choke. Same applies here. In many ways, use of ChatGPT as a generative writing tool is responsive to writing instruction that values exact language over exploratory writing, emphasizing a correct final product over a messy writing process. Here, again, is the case of sounding academic rather than learning to develop writing practices that cross genres and disciplines–a demand for immediacy rather than a nurturing of authenticity.

ENGLISHES (PLURAL)

Tonouchi's (2004) primary focus in penning "Da State of Pidgin Address"[10] moves far beyond only confronting academic mimicry. The article is grounded in another set of troubling circumstances when students are asked to conform to a discursive norm: language supremacy that contributes to racism, xenophobia, and linguisticism, the unfair treatment of people based on their language or dialect. In one scene, he talked about the shame students feel when their written and/or spoken language falls outside the strict confines of *Academic English*[11] that is positioned as the *standard*: "Dey say if you talk Pidgin you no can be smart, important, [or] successful…; "you no can be [a] teacher, doctor, [or] lawyer…" (p. 77) "Dey say if you talk Pidgin YOU NO CAN" (p. 79). In the writing classroom, these voices are commonly silenced just the same, the result of a misguided belief that students who enter colleges and universities share a *common* form of English (Matsuda, 2006). This "myth of linguistic homogeneity" leads to the belief that there is a *correct* English that all students must adopt, resulting in linguistic diversity going unacknowledged, which marginalizes some students while privileging others (Matsuda, 2006; Lyiscott, 2019). Such myths about the teaching and learning of writing also construct and perpetuate a linguistic hierarchy based on "conquest and domination" (hooks, 1994, p.168), a contributing factor to institutional practices that reject African American Vernacular English (AAVE) for example, and uphold white linguistic supremacy by positioning AAVE and those who speak it as inferior (Kynard, 2007; Baker-Bell, 2020). Language prejudice, of course, is not limited to Pidgin or AAVE speakers and includes people who "talk and write Asian or black or with an Applachian accent or sound like whatever aint the status quo" (Young, 2010, p. 110). Standard English "is the mask that hides the loss of so many tongues, all those sounds of diverse, native communities we will never hear, the speech of the Gullah, Yiddish, and so many other unremembered tongues"(hooks, 1994, p.168).

Required imitation of standard English, the *parody* mentioned above, is more complex and controversial than my initial explanations led on. While still an expectation that limits writing/writer development, it is a judgment based not on skill or ability but rather on prejudice. Its enforcement disregards years of research and established field best practices, including the Conference of College Composition and Communication (CCCC) statement, "Students' Rights to Their Own Language" (1974):

> We affirm the students' right to their own patterns and varieties of language -- the dialects of their nurture or whatever dialects in which they find their own identity and style. Language scholars long ago denied that the myth

---

10 Speech developed out of communicative necessity between people who do not share a common language.
11 Formal language used in academic settings, such as universities, research, scholarly publications, and professional environments. Critics have argued that it is biased, exclusionary, and hierarchical.

of a standard American dialect has any validity. The claim that any one dialect is unacceptable amounts to an attempt of one social group to exert its dominance over another. Such a claim leads to false advice for speakers and writers, and immoral advice for humans... ("Explanation of Adoption")

In line with "This Ain't Another Statement! This is a Demand for Black Linguistic Justice," we do not advocate that students *code-switch*, a form of writing instruction that removes all language considered outside the standard from the public, including the classroom (CCCC, 2020). In other words, students are frequently compelled and coerced to leave their authentic voices at home and speak "properly" at school (Young, 2010, p. 114). Instead, we follow the lead and direction of Keith Gilyard (1991), Geneva Smitherman (1996), Vershawn Ashanti Young (2010, 2014), Aja Y. Martinez (2022), and many other BIPOC scholars to create inclusive spaces where all languages and dialects are valued. Rather than "code-switching," we advocate for "code-meshing," what Young et al. (2014) defined as a "blending of dialects and languages, allowing people to speak and write in a way that acknowledges their multiple linguistic identities" (p. 6). In short, code-meshing undermines the system and practices in which students give up their elegant and nuanced languages and dialects in order to *sound smart*. Such a strange premise, right? To sound smart, one needs to sound less like themselves, as if they are not smart already. To *come as you are* is to be unconstrained, to write and speak clearly, directly, and proudly, with sincerity, security, and most importantly, a sense of self. Part of coming to higher education *as you are* is directly and intimately connected to language usage. How you speak and write–your dialect, accent, vernacular, and register–reflect aspects of your social and cultural identities. As instructors, we honor this multiplicity.

THE SELF AND THE SOCIAL

While advocates for centering the individual in academic writing, we as a program realize that the self is not exclusive to the individual person. If that sounds a bit strange, let me explain. Thinking about or discussing who we are is to consider identity, which includes personal, social, and cultural ways of knowing ourselves that are constructed and mediated by language. So, while we cultivate individual or personal identities over time, we must also be aware that these markers or characteristics are formed in and by social and cultural forces, as who we interact with and what comes from those interactions play a large role in how we perceive ourselves and others, along with how we ourselves are perceived. Writers must avoid mistakenly isolating the self from the social or social from the self, seeing one separate from the other. Rather, as feminist writer Carol Hanisch (2006) made famous in her essay of the same name, the "personal is political," that is to say that our personal experiences and identities, while unique, take shape from (and also shape) social, cultural, economic, and political forces.

One form of identity does not need to be sacrificed for another. We can engage the self without losing local, national, and global perspectives just as we can engage with sociocultural phenomena, not at the expense of the personal. What is important to understand, what I want to stress, is that writing stems from the self in one way or another but does not have to directly address the individual experience. In other words, all writing, regardless of genre, generates from the self. We write and communicate with a purpose, not by happenstance, a concept you will learn about in Katherine Dye's Chapter 4 contribution to this text: "Toward an Understanding of Writing and Rhetoric." What we say, why and how we say it, and for what purpose is driven by the individual.

At times, as is the case in a personal narrative, the self is evident through the use of the first-person pronoun. Other writing, such as content, discourse, or rhetorical analysis, focuses on source material and not individual experience, and while the author may not write in the first-person, they are still very much on the page (or they should be). The argument writers make, persuasive tactics they utilize, sources they select, and the analysis they include are all indicative of their individual presence. How writers are positioned or position themselves is simply the result of genre expectations. But, make no mistake about it, nothing happens on autopilot. The writer is always orchestrating and directing their writing.

DISCOURSE COMMUNITIES

Joseph Harris (1989), who also was in dialogue with Elbow and Bartholomae, observed that people write as "members of communities whose beliefs, concerns, and practices both instigate and constrain...the sorts of things [they] can say" (p. 12). As such, social and cultural interactions take place in "discourse communities," a term Jack Morales will further explain in Chapter 2, "Entering Academic Discourse Communities." For now, I will review the basics. To understand what constitutes a discourse community, I want to first make clear that students are already members before even entering a college writing classroom. Their homes and hobbies, social media pages and text chats, signal belonging to such communities. According to the scholarship of James Paul Gee (1990):

> A Discourse is a socially accepted association among ways of using language, of thinking, feeling, believing, valuing, and of acting that can be used to identify oneself as a member of a socially meaningful group or social network, or to signal (that one is playing) a socially meaningful role. (p. 143)

Discourse, therefore, places language into a social context in which it is used to convey identity, belief, and social practices, what Gee (1989) called an "identity kit"- a way of performing and communicating that others recognize given the expectations of time and place (p. 7). Adding the word "community" highlights how groups of people use shared language to establish collective values and meet common goals (Swales, 1990). This brings us back to Bartholomae (1986), who saw writing classes as a discourse community, one in which students learn a specialized language and particular ways of structuring that communication to meet existing academic expectations.

And again, I do not have any issue with helping students engage with a variety of discourses; this is important and necessary work in which writers consider writing expectations and conventions as being less general and more localized (Bizzell, 1992). As a matter of fact, the Pace, Pleasantville writing program is shaped by discourse communities. In ENG 110: Composition, students study the university and education more broadly to determine how institutional histories, discourses, and rhetorics shape the writing process.

In other words, first-year writing is a discourse community. That said, I am concerned when students are urged to take on an identity or persona that is not yet their own in a language that Bartholomae claimed to be "dynamic" but is, in fact "fixed," shifting "from something a writer must continually reinvent to something that has already been invented…" (Harris, 1989, p. 13). I have never been a fan of style over substance, and that is just what I hear when students are compelled to enter a dialogue without having the time to determine what they actually think and how they would like to convey those thoughts. I am far more intrigued by critical thinking in a language that is natural than trivialized in incomprehensible writing.

Rather than placing discourses at odds with one another, we as a program believe that students "might better be encouraged towards a kind of polyphony–an awareness of and pleasure in the various competing discourses that make up their own" (Harris, 1989, p. 17). The self and the community are not mutually exclusive. Through insight and imagination, communities take shape and evolve. Otherwise, they would simply circulate the same information, through the same language, in the same patterns. Luckily, as we can see from the tracing of any group of people, what they know and how they convey that knowledge is always evolving, a testament to the relationship between the individual and community at large.

WRITING TO LEARN AND LEARNING TO WRITE

To *come as you are* does not mean that students will leave the class the same way that they had entered it. Writing functions as a tool of discovery instead of being what is discovered. The latter is the result of a decontextualized *skill and drill* process in which students learn to write in an isolated, disjointed, and disconnected manner that leads to formulaic rather than authentic writing and writers. In our classes, *writing to learn* is paramount and carries with it several meanings: learning about a specific topic, generating an individualized writing process, and developing a language of writing that fosters internal and external communication about creation and revision, topics that will be discussed in Chapter 3: "Forging a Writing Process" by Christina Gonzalez and Chapter 7: "Engaging Writers in a Dialogue of Revision" by Zac Ginsburg.

Writing to learn, therefore, precedes writing to show mastery[12], which is often, and incorrectly, the first and final product of standardized education and testing that is all too common in contemporary schooling, a system that leaves students confused, frustrated, and, above all, terrified of making a mistake[13]. Error, in fact, is directly related to learning. When drafting, we are trying for the first time to figure it out–find our way into a conversation that is not yet our own. Sentences run on and thoughts collide. Ideas start and stop abruptly. Arguments take shape and trail off. Organization is disjointed. Perhaps Anne Lamott (2005) said it best: "For me and most of the other writers I know, writing is not rapturous. In fact, the only way I can get anything written at all is to write really, really shitty first drafts" (p. 1). Even after considerable revisions, writing rarely renders a product that is fully fleshed out, pristine, and polished–and that is just fine.

---

12 Writing that demonstrates expertise and authority on a subject.
13 In Chapter 1: "Mapping the Academic Terraine Between High School and College Writing," Justine Matias discusses the shifting writing practices and expectations students face when entering a college writing classroom.

Writing to learn and writing to show mastery cannot be completed simultaneously; rather, they need to be scaffolded in a manner that allows sufficient time for students to consider the task at hand and pathways into the assignment that value genuine interest and inquiry. Our writing builds and builds and builds again until degrees of genre, rhetorical, and/or content proficiency begin organically taking shape. Writing is rarely a linear act and instead is refined through revision and reflection, terms that are expanded upon in Chapter 3. To facilitate a classroom dynamic in which students feel comfortable, one that is conducive to personal growth, instructors serve as guides to writing autonomy and authenticity. Through a series of assignments, drafts, conferences, and workshops, students explore writing as an experiential and recursive process[14] of action and reflection, a practice of ongoing discovery that involves thinking, experimenting, and refining (Murray, 1972). Writing to learn is part of a process-based pedagogy that values why and how students approach writing, which is commonly overlooked when the final writing product supersedes the process taken to create that work. It is a metacognitive exercise in which students begin to discover how they learn and how they write by critically and continually thinking about their thinking, considering what they are doing, why they are doing it, and how successful they are as a result.

The writing process is interactive, even communal, not work done alone in isolation. And as such, it requires a specific form of communication, what we call the "language of writing." This language is the result of writing to learn, as it grows from the time spent developing and adjusting how we approach writing. Through a process-based practice, students develop as deliberate and intentional writers and readers, those who make decisions based on experience not decontextualized writing instruction. As students progress as writers, this language does the same, moving from ambiguity to specificity. During instructor and peer workshops, this language allows students to work from within texts and not outside of them, building on what they know of themselves as writers and applying that thinking when critically reviewing their own work or giving feedback to peers. For students to be inside their own or their classmate's writing means to speak clearly and precisely. Such language avoids general statements that offer little direction ("it lacks flow") and instead considers feedback from higher to lower order concerns, moving from fluency to clarity and culminating with correctness. Since writing is practiced throughout the university and workforce, intention and awareness are essential for writing transfer, the ability to apply what has been learned in one context to another. Developing a language of writing and being able to transfer that practice according to task, audience, and genre expectations allows students to be thoughtful and confident communicators who are prepared to thoroughly engage as writers across academic disciplines and professional fields.

LABOR-BASED GRADES

Filling the page should be a heuristic exercise in which students seek to learn from a sense of intrinsic need and value and not extrinsic validation. This can be a hard sell to students who have spent years in classrooms where grades served as what motivated

---

14 Recursive writing is the cyclical practice of reviewing, revising, and reflecting throughout each stage of the writing process.

learning (Inman & Powell, 2018; Kryger & Zimmerman, 2020). Our commitment to students is to both provide them time to learn about themselves as writers and grade them according to their progress and growth as opposed to meeting a single marker of success that "reserve[s] the highest scores for 'good' writers [and not] engaged students (Mundy & Hantgan, 2024, "Tracking Labor"). Much of our approach to grading is informed by Asao Inoue (2023), who has written extensively about Labor Based Grades (LBG), an assessment approach that evaluates students based on the effort and time they put into their work rather than the quality or correctness of the final product. Thinking back to the earlier section, "Englishes (Plural)," we can see the connection between LBG and inclusivity, as this grading practice values the process and engagement of all students, regardless of their prior educational backgrounds or relationship with standard English (Inoue, 2023). Traci Gardner (n.d.) has drawn attention to the more practical nature of LBG, in which students are afforded the freedom to "focus on ideas (not mistakes)," "write for [themselves] (not [the professor])," and "take risks (don't play it safe)," all of which serve to reduce anxiety and increase writing production and creativity ("When Your Grades"). As I have written in the past with my co-editor Alysa Hantgan, "honoring labor...reflects a [true] commitment to process pedagogy"(Mundy & Hantgan, 2024, "Tracking Labor") and student agency.

ALT WRITING STUDIES

As a writer, I have never been fond of bookending my work or, better said, explicitly making that connection between its beginning and closing. If the writing is good, the initial thought should linger ever so slightly on each page. It stays on task but moves forward toward new ideas, not back to where it started. This chapter feels different, though, since it is based on a specific phrase from a specific time that serves as the ethos of a specific class and writing program. For these reasons, please indulge me as I make my case for the spirit of alternative rock helping to shape the writing classroom.

I will save you the extended history and say this: grunge, along with the associated constellation of alt subgenres, including indie rock, Riot Grrrl, post-punk, college rock, and noise rock, did away with past music excess and opted for a punk aesthetic, a do it yourself (DIY) mindset that was about access and not gatekeeping. If you had something to say – start a band and project your voice out to the masses. What interests me and what informs this book, along with my teaching, about this intersection of music and writing is what it stood for and what it can and should stand for in our classes. The music of that era was about honest and raw authenticity. Its stripped-down approach brought with it an intimacy and vulnerability between artist and audience. Lyrics challenged social, cultural, and political norms, subverting antiquated thoughts, advocating empowerment, and embracing change.

I hope you can see, as I do, the connections between this chapter and its conclusion. To come as you are and to write from that position requires a fair amount of candor and earnestness. It asks you to strip away much of what you have been taught about writing to develop an authentic understanding and practice of communication. Your prose does not need to be glossy or overmanufactured to the point of which who you are and what you have to say is no longer distinguishable on the page. Reject all of that. Fiercely dedicate yourself to the creative process and wherever that takes you. Confidently place your thoughts, emotions, and experiences into words, your words. Know that we, the faculty, are eager to hear your stories and help you locate them in ongoing and circulating language that shapes our collective days and lives. Come as you are / as you were / as you want to be.

REFERENCES

Baker-Bell, A. (2020). Linguistic justice: Black language, literacy, identity, and pedagogy. Routledge & National Council of Teachers of English.

Bartholomae, D. (1986). Inventing the university. Journal of Basic Writing, 5(1), 4-23. https://doi.org/10.37514/JBW-J.1986.5.1.02

Bizzell, P. (1992). Academic Discourse and Critical Consciousness. University of Pittsburgh Press.

Cobain, K. (1991). Come as you are [Song]. On Nevermind [Album]. DGC Records.

Elbow, P. (1995). Being a writer vs. being an academic: A conflict of goals. College Composition and Communication, 46(1), 72-83. https://doi.org/10.2307/358871

Freire, P. (2000). Pedagogy of the oppressed (M.B. Ramos, Trans.) Continuum. (Original work published 1968)

Gardner, T. (n.d.). When your grades are based on labor. https://tracigardner.com/labor/

Gee, J. P. (1990). Social linguistics and literacies: Ideology in discourses. London: Falmer Press. Gilyard, K. (1991). Voices of the self: A study of language competence. Wayne State University Press.

Hanish, C. (1970). The personal is political. In S. Firestone & A. Koedt (Eds.), Notes from the second year: Women's liberation (pp. 76-77). Radical Feminism.

Hantgan, A. R., & Mundy, R. (2024, August 5). Beyond the single classroom: A model for program-wide alternative grading. Beyond the Single Classroom: A Model for Program-Wide Alternative Grading. https://gradingforgrowth.com/p/beyond-the-single-classroom-a-model

Harris, J. (1989). The idea of community in the study of writing. College Composition and Communication, 40(1), 11-22. https://doi.org/10.2307/358177

hooks, b. (1994). Teaching to transgress: Education as the practice of freedom. Routledge.

Inman, J. O. & Powell, R. A. (2020). In the absence of grades. Conference on College Composition and Communication, 7(1), 30-56. https://www.jstor.org/stable/10.2307/26772544

Inoue, A. B. (2023). Labor-based grading contracts: Building Equity and inclusion in the compassionate classroom. WAC Clearinghouse.

Kryger, K. & Zimmerman, G. X. neurodivergence and intersectionality in labor-based grading contracts. Journal of Writing Assessment, 12(2), https://escholarship.org/uc/item/0934x4rm

Kynard, C. (2007). "I want to be African": In search of a Black radical tradition/African-American-vernacularized paradigm for "Students' right to their own language," critical literacy, and "class politics." College English, 69(4), 360–90.

Lamott, A. (2005). Shitty first drafts. In P. Eschholz, A. Rosa, & V. Clark (Eds.), Language awareness: Readings for college writers (pp. 93-96). Boston: Bedford/St. Martin.

Lyiscott, J. (2019). Black appetite. White food: Issues of race, voice, and justice within and beyond the classroom. Routledge.

Martinez, A. Y. (2022). Counterstory: The rhetoric and writing of critical race theory. Conference on College Composition and Communication, National Council of Teachers of English.

Matsuda, P. E. (2006). The myth of linguistic homogeneity in U.S. college composition. College English, 68(6), 637-651. https://doi.org/10.2307/25472180

Murray, D. (1984). Write to learn. Harcourt College Publishers.

Perl, S. (1979). The composing processes of unskilled college writers. Research in the Teaching of English, 13(4), 317-336. https://www.jstor.org/stable/40170774

Rider, J. (1991). Must imitation be the mother of invention? Journal of Teaching Writing, 9(2), 175-185.

Rodríguez, R. J. (2017). Leave yourself out of your writing. In C.E. Ball & D.M. Loewe (Eds.) Bad ideas about writing (pp. 131-133).

Smitherman, G. (1996). Talkin and testifyin: The Language of Black America. Wayne State University. Press.

Students' right to their own language (1974). Conference on College Composition and Communication. https://cccc.ncte.org/cccc/resources/positions/srtolsummary

Swales, J. M. (1990). Genre analysis: English in academic and research settings. Cambridge UP.

Tonouchi, L. A. (2004). Da state of pidgin address. College English, 67(1), 75-82. https://doi.org/10.2307/4140726

Young, V. A. Should writers use they own English? Iowa Journal of Cultural Studies, 12(1), 110-117. https://doi.org/10.17077/2168-569X.1095

Young, V. A., Barrett, R., Young-Rivera, Y., & Lovejoy, K. B. (2014). Other people's English: Code-meshing, code-switching, and African American literacy. Teachers College Press.

SECTION ONE:
WRITING FOUNDATIONS

CHAPTER 1

MAPPING THE ACADEMIC TERRAINE BETWEEN HIGH SCHOOL AND COLLEGE WRITING

Justine Matias

CHAPTER OUTCOMES

- Reflect on the value of your prior writing experiences.
- Compare high school and college writing expectations.
- Describe writing skills learned in high school that will apply in the first-year writing classroom.

KEY TERMS

- First-Year Writing
- Academic Literacy
- Collaborative Writing

CHAPTER OVERVIEW

This chapter aims to clarify not only the assumptions of writing that you and your peers may have when transitioning from high school to college but also to provide you with the necessary information needed for what you can expect in your first-year Writing (FYW) course. As writing instructors, we want to assure students that their prior experience with writing in high school provides a foundational context yet highlights the key differences you can expect at the college level. Beyond FYW courses, you will encounter diverse writing expectations across disciplines (college courses/majors), requiring adaptability and rhetorical awareness. Emphasizing the importance of reading rhetorically, instructors will guide you when analyzing texts critically and recognizing the nuances of audience, purpose, genre, and context. Moreover, you are now part of a vibrant community of writers where collaboration, peer feedback, and engagement with diverse perspectives enrich the writing process. This chapter provides insight into navigating the complexities of college-level writing while leveraging your existing skills and experiences.

FROM HIGH SCHOOL TO COLLEGE

When transitioning from high school to FYW, you will encounter a dynamic shift where your prior experiences and contexts play a significant role. Each and every one of you brings a unique array of backgrounds and prior writing encounters, shaping your approach to academic writing. Recognizing this diversity is crucial (although not always blatantly evident), as it empowers you to embrace your individuality in your writing journey. While some may have extensive experience in formal writing settings, others may be less familiar with academic conventions, and that is fine. Either way, throughout your college career (especially in your FYW course), you will all learn the necessary skills and techniques to build upon what you already know, to help build and expand your writing. By encouraging you to embrace your distinct perspectives and capabilities and by building upon the skills you already possess, this approach fosters a more inclusive and supportive environment for academic growth.

It's crucial to recognize the valuable foundation that high school writing provides while also acknowledging the differences you will encounter in college. Many students enter college with the assumption that the writing conventions and expectations they learned in high school will seamlessly translate into their college-level work. While high school writing certainly equips you with fundamental skills such as grammar, structure, and basic argumentation, FYW introduces new dimensions such as critical analysis, independent research, and disciplinary-specific conventions. Thus, approaching your FYW course with an open mind is important for recognizing that while your high school experiences have laid the groundwork, you must also be willing to adapt and expand your writing practices to meet the demands of higher education. Studies in the field confirm what we already know from experience: that students will find writing in college to be quite different from what they did in high school (Crank, 2012). These studies delve into how these variations make the shift from high school writing to college writing more challenging. No longer will you write only for English courses like you did in high school, but instead, college prepares you for writing across multiple curriculums.

FYW extends beyond literary analysis and the five-paragraph essay. In college, writing transcends disciplinary boundaries and permeates various courses and fields of study. FYW is meant to engage you with the course material, assisting you in formulating your own ideas and thoughts pertaining to what you are learning. For instance, I remember my first college history class, where instead of being quizzed on important dates and political figures, I was asked to write a research paper analyzing and synthesizing sources on the social injustice against immigrants. Or in my biology course, where I thought tests were the only source of assessing our knowledge, my instructor (to my surprise) asked us to compose lab reports detailing experimental procedures and findings. It was then when I realized that writing was happening across all of my classes and not just in a FYW course, as previously assumed.

Since writing does not take place solely in the confines of a FYW course, writing becomes multifaceted, where you and your peers must adapt your writing styles and formats to meet the specific demands of each discipline (course). In return, this prepares you for the diverse writing tasks you will encounter in your academic and professional pursuits. The skills you hone in on or acquire in your FYW course will provide you with the necessary skills needed to read, comprehend, and write in other courses throughout your college career. During a time of really big changes, writing is set to watch and join in on figuring out and making new ideas in different subjects and how we make knowledge (Yood, 2012). Overall, transitioning to FYW entails adapting to higher expectations, embracing intellectual challenges, and developing the skills necessary for success in higher education and beyond.

COLLEGE WRITING

Rather than solely emphasizing the end result (a final draft of a high-stakes assignment), FYW places significant importance on the iterative writing process, including brainstorming, drafting, revising, and editing. This paradigm shift encourages you to engage deeply with your writing, exploring ideas, refining arguments, and experimenting with different rhetorical strategies. Moreover, FYW courses often incorporate peer review and instructor feedback as integral components, fostering collaboration and reflective practices that promote continual growth and improvement as writers. The process of writing happens in different steps and does not need to start or end in a specific place on the page. In my FYW courses, I encourage students to brainstorm ideas in many different ways. In small assigned groups, my students can bounce ideas off of each other through conversation. When they work independently, perhaps they are freewriting first (writing freely by jotting down whatever comes to mind), or making an outline. Then, after they write some words down on paper, I like to conference one-on-one with my students to discuss their ideas and make a plan for future writing. Usually, we go back and forth between brainstorming, writing, and conferencing multiple times before a draft is even produced. Either way, whatever "system" you or your instructor have when it comes to writing, your FYW course will help you develop stronger writing skills so you can cultivate a deeper understanding of yourselves as writers and critical thinkers.

Writing is recursive, meaning that each step you take in your writing process will filter over into other steps. For example, your teacher asks you to write a research essay on a topic of your choice. First you begin to brainstorm topics, then you conduct preliminary research, and finally you start writing an essay. Some students believe that they're finished writing once the essay has been submitted for a grade, but that is not always the case. Writing does not end the moment you submit your essay. You will likely have to conduct peer reviews and have conferences with your instructor or a writing consultant at the Writing Center, which then lead you to return to your first draft and revise/edit to produce a stronger version of your original essay. This is what we call a recursive process of writing because writing is a process- it is not linear.

When writing in college, you will experience how writing goes beyond just putting words down on paper. Writing is a way for you to express yourself- the prior knowledge you already cultivated from previous experiences mixed in with the knowledge you are obtaining from current experiences (school, work, and/or personal life). Writing across curriculums allows you to interject yourself into the conversation. Instructors want to see your own voice in your writing. They want to get to know your ideas, your thoughts, how you understand and perceive information. A huge part of college is finding your true identity and who you are and want to be in the real world. In order to do that, you need to use your own voice in your writing. For new students who are always changing, writing acts like a mirror. It shows them who they are as students, letting them see themselves through their own words (Sommers & Saltz, 2004).

Writing in college means writing across different genres and for different audiences. In high school, you were very much focused on writing either a response to a text or a five-paragraph essay to your teacher and peers. However, in college you are encouraged (and sometimes even required) to write different types of assignments to a vast array of audiences. When students finish high school and begin college, they usually do not know much about the different types of writing and how to use them for different purposes. Instead of learning this, they often stick to simple rules that help them think but might not be the best for the people reading their work (Crank, 2012). High school composition often revolves around mastering basic writing skills, such as crafting cohesive paragraphs and structuring essays according to a standardized format. Your assignments were tailored to meet specific curriculum standards and were primarily geared towards demonstrating comprehension of course material and developing critical thinking skills within a controlled academic environment.

In contrast, FYW demands a more sophisticated approach, requiring you to engage with a diverse array of genres and audiences. College-level writing tasks encompass research papers, scientific reports, persuasive speeches, and professional correspondence such as letters, emails, and memos, among others. Moreover, college writing encourages you to adapt your style and tone to suit different disciplinary conventions and target audiences, fostering versatility and adaptability in communication skills. The transition from high school to FYW thus entails not only mastering different genres but also navigating the complexities of diverse rhetorical situations. If you are unfamiliar with the writing conventions across vast genres, do not fret. You are already equipped with the necessary skills needed and your FYW instructor will assist you every step of the way in case you need help. Every semester, when I ask my students to write an essay for an audience member other than myself (their instructor), they all give me their best confused look: eyebrows furrowed, heads tilted to the side as if they're all saying, "Huh?" simultaneously. My students usually do not have experience writing an essay for anyone other than their teacher, so it always comes as a surprise when I ask for an essay to be written to an author of a text we just read or even to a family member. This is where your FYW courses will help develop those skills that you may not have a lot of experience with.

READ, READ, AND THEN READ SOME MORE...

Reading and writing definitely go hand in hand (as you have learned throughout your entire academic career) and are both critical aspects to being successful not only in college but in your professional lives. Reading with a purpose consists of knowing what you are looking for before you dive into the text. Are you reading to summarize? To evaluate? To critique? As a high school student, you were trained to read in order to find specific answers to very specific questions, to look for keywords that would help save time when it came to standardized testing. In college, you are taught to read in a broader sense, where you take everything that's written into consideration in order to formulate your own ideas on the topic at hand. In college, reading is not just about understanding the main idea but about breaking down texts to see how different parts connect (Horning & Kraemer, 2013). You will need to combine various readings about the same topic to understand different viewpoints or research. Afterward, you must assess the materials critically in order to use said material for your own needs and goals.

Reading comprehension is more than just understanding the words on the page; it involves actively engaging with the text to extract meaning, analyze arguments, and evaluate evidence. Effective reading comprehension requires you to employ a range of strategies, including annotating, summarizing, questioning, and making connections between ideas. You should also be aware of the importance of context in interpreting texts, considering factors such as the author's background, purpose, and intended audience. Additionally, as

FYW students, you should recognize that reading is a recursive process (just like writing), meaning that revisiting texts, seeking clarification, and reflecting on one's understanding are essential for deepening comprehension over time. When a basic writer gets better at understanding what they read, it means they're starting to grasp a piece of writing and all its parts, as part of, or in response to, ongoing discussions (Skomski, 2013). It is imperative to understand that reading comprehension is a skill that can be developed and honed through practice, persistence, and an openness to new ideas and perspectives.

COMPOSITION AS A COMMUNITY

In the context of First-Year Writing (FYW), the distinction between writing as a solitary activity and writing as a communal endeavor is crucial. FYW emphasizes the social aspect of writing, providing you with opportunities to engage with a community of writers rather than working in isolation. By participating in peer workshops, collaborative projects, and group discussions, you will learn to navigate the complexities of academic discourse within a supportive and interactive environment. When you engage in collaborative writing environments, you benefit from diverse perspectives, constructive feedback, and collective problem-solving. This collaborative approach not only enhances the quality of individual writing but also fosters a sense of belonging and inclusion within the academic community. Moreover, writing as a communal activity reflects larger social dynamics, emphasizing the importance of cooperation, empathy, and mutual respect. By working together, you learn to appreciate the value of collaboration and develop essential skills for navigating complex social and professional relationships beyond the classroom. In this way, writing as a community not only enriches the learning experience but also prepares you to contribute meaningfully to broader societal conversations and endeavors.

In college, writing undergoes a fundamental shift from the relative solitude of high school compositions. Unlike the individualized approach often associated with high school writing assignments, FYW is inherently communal. The focus broadens from the isolated writer to an interactive, participatory community. In high school, assignments might have been completed within the confines of a singular perspective, with minimal external input. In contrast, college writing demands active engagement with a diverse community of peers, instructors, and resources. Through collaborative projects, group discussions, and peer reviews, you will not only refine your own ideas but also contribute to a larger tapestry of shared knowledge. The communal nature of college writing fosters a dynamic environment where the exchange of ideas not only sharpens individual skills but also enriches the collective understanding of the subject matter. As you transition from the more solitary writing practices of high school to the collaborative ethos of college, you will find yourself immersed in a vibrant intellectual dialogue that extends far beyond the confines of personal perspectives. Embrace the diversity of voices and perspectives around you, for it is within this collective exchange that your own voice will find resonance and depth.

CONCLUSION

The transition from high school to FYW marks a significant shift in both approach and expectation. This chapter has aimed to illuminate the differences between these two realms of writing while also emphasizing the importance of adaptation and growth. As you embark on your college journey, remember that your prior experiences in high school writing provide a foundational context, but FYW courses introduce new dimensions and challenges. From embracing diverse writing expectations across disciplines to understanding the iterative nature of the writing process, your FYW experience will be multifaceted and dynamic. Moreover, the communal nature of FYW underscores the significance of collaboration, peer feedback, and engagement with diverse perspectives. By navigating the complexities of college-level writing while leveraging your existing skills and experiences, you will not only thrive academically but also contribute meaningfully to broader intellectual and societal conversations. Welcome to the vibrant community of writers, where your voice matter and your journey toward academic and personal growth begins.

In the upcoming chapters, you will learn everything you need to transition smoothly into your college career. By actively engaging in practice and understanding the processes applicable to your own writing, you'll not only enhance your skills but also develop a deeper sense of confidence in your abilities. Moreover, recognizing the importance of your experiences, interests, and backgrounds will empower you to bring authenticity to your writing, enriching both your voice and perspective. Embracing support systems, trying new approaches, and welcoming feedback will further foster your growth and evolution as a writer. Ultimately, through these chapters, you'll embark on a journey of self-discovery, gaining insights into your unique identity and voice as you navigate the diverse landscapes of writing. So, let's embark on this transformative journey together, armed with curiosity, resilience, and a passion for exploration.

DISCUSSION QUESTIONS AND ACTIVITIES

1. How do you think the transition from high school to college writing differs from other academic transitions, such as transitioning between different courses or majors?
2. Reflect on a specific experience you had with writing in high school and compare it to what you've learned about college-level writing expectations. What similarities and differences do you notice?
3. How do you think the concept of writing as a communal activity influences the way we approach writing in college?
4. Write a brief reflection on your own experiences, interests, and backgrounds, and consider how these factors influence your writing voice and perspective. Share your reflection with a partner and discuss any commonalities or differences in your writing experiences.
5. Choose a piece of writing from your high school portfolio and analyze it in terms of its structure, argumentation, and audience. Then, imagine how you would revise it to meet the expectations of a FYW course.

REFERENCES

Crank, V. (2012). From high school to college: Developing writing skills in the disciplines. The WAC Journal, 23(1), 49–63. https://doi.org/10.37514/wac-j.2012.23.1.04
    Horning, A.S. & Kraemer, E.W. (2013). Reconnecting reading and writing: Introduction and overview. In A. S. Horning & E. W. Kraemer (Eds.), Reconnecting reading and writing (pp. 5-25). Parlor

Press Parlor Press; The WAC Clearinghouse. https://wac.colostate.edu/books/referenceguides/reconnecting/

Skomski, K. (2013). first-year writers: Forward movement, backward progress.

Sommers, N., & Saltz, L. (2004). The novice as expert: Writing the freshman year. College Composition and Communication, 56(1), 124-149. https://doi.org/10.2307/4140684

Yood, J. (2005). Present-process: The composition of change. Journal of Basic Writing, 24(2), 4–25. https://doi.org/10.37514/jbw-j.2005.24.2.02

CHAPTER 2

ENTERING ACADEMIC DISCOURSE COMMUNITIES

Jack N. Morales

CHAPTER OUTCOMES

- Explain the concept of a discourse community.
- Identify and apply the characteristics of a discourse community.
- Differentiate between local, focal, and "fo-local" discourse communities.

KEY TERMS

- Discourse Community
- Local Discourse Community
- Focal Discourse Community
- Fo-local Discourse Community
- Regulation
- Socialization
- Certification
- Culture of Endorsement and Sponsorship

CHAPTER OVERVIEW

The university is a discourse community (DC). In other words, it is a social space that we learn to navigate through practices that shape our membership over time. At least two of those practices – reading and writing – are a part of your daily membership in a group that relies on language to establish, define, and regulate the social conditions of even smaller DCs called "disciplines." In this chapter, you will learn about the nature of a DC, a little about its history and theory, and how to think about this as you learn to navigate more than one while a student at Pace.

ALLEGORY OF AN AUTOMOBILE

I was a late bloomer when it came to learning something that most of my friends knew how to do by the time I got to college. That something was driving a car. Even though many of them didn't have one, almost everyone I knew in my friend group had a driver's license. I was the only one – or so I thought – to have a state-issued "non-driver" ID. It would be about a dozen years or so until I found myself in a borrowed car with an agent from the local DMV, looking down at the clipboard and checking off the boxes indicating all of the mistakes I was making in the road test. I was feeling confident, though. By then, I had passed the Pennsylvania Department of Transportation's (PennDOT) written exam, I had my picture taken, and I was given a temporary license which allowed me to drive a car as long as someone with an official driver's license was present. None of these things, however, made me feel any less scared that I might get into an accident during the road test or that the examiner might be unsatisfied with my performance and, therefore, fail me on the spot. Even parallel parking, the quintessential skill of an officially sanctioned driver, filled me with dread that day. When it was all said and done, I passed the exam with points taken off for driving too slowly on a one-lane country road.

In the months that followed, official driver's license in hand, I drove under the speed limit to work. I avoided the parkway, onramps, or any bend in the road that looked too complicated to navigate. Roads with right angles were my friends. Although I lived 25 minutes from my campus, it would take me 45 (60 if there was traffic) to travel to work. My first-year writing students at the time would talk to me about shortcuts to campus and when they were feeling very courageous, they would ask why I don't just take the parkway. I told them the truth. I was afraid of getting into an accident while using the onramp.

Ironically, we had switched roles. They were counseling me on my fears of learning and trying something new, a skill I had seen others perform masterfully. I had seen friends, partners, and family talk on the phone, eat a hamburger, and make gestures of thanks and anger toward other drivers. What eluded me was being able to get on the parkway by using the crowded onramp, a proposition that filled me with dread. One day, Steven – a student in my research writing class – asked me how the driving was going. They listened as I would describe taking the streets rather than the highway and that one day, I will feel comfortable enough to use the onramp. Steven thought for a minute and said something I thought was brilliant: "nothing can prepare you for the highway", he said, "just remember that you're part of a system and your blinker lets people know you want to join". His answer was rooted in the belief that other drivers would see me and make room. Anyone who drives knows that this is true...sometimes.

I offer this story as an introduction to this chapter because I think it encapsulates concepts that could help us – as students and teachers of writing – to understand why writing can seem so easy one day and so difficult the next. It's also kind of an allegory for what many of us learn about school: that it is a primarily private affair between you and your own goals. We learn over the years that the purpose of writing seems to be to perform our identities as students. We demonstrate our awareness of "good writing" by doing it in ways that are considered acceptable by our high school English teacher or our college writing professors who in turn might use their identities to represent standard correctness in style and grammar. They might mark our papers not as individuals with their own ideas about writing but as representatives of "the standard" or of social propriety. It is their embodied expertise which persuades us that we're "good" or "bad" writers. We depend on them – unhealthily, maybe – to bestow us with the idea that we belong in college, not because everyone is entitled to have a space in college to learn and grow intellectually but because we know how to speak, read, and write in acceptable ways. By the time we get to college, we've internalized this system so that it feels natural to think of writing as something we're "good at" or that we "like."

Now, before I break any more of the rules of good writing, let me finally get to the thesis of this essay. I argue, here, that being successful at writing as a university student is about learning what a university is, how it works, and the role writing plays in helping you establish your membership in the communities and groups that make up that space. To do this, I will offer up a tentative definition of something called a discourse community, a concept that has its origins in the field of applied linguistics and that is now a regular part of the specialized vocabulary of the field of rhetoric and writing studies. The concept foregrounds what is most important to understand about life at Pace, or any other university for that matter: that its social and linguistic boundaries – both real and imagined – shape our everyday lives on and off campus. We learn very quickly, for example, how to navigate and interpret our relationship to our classes through a "Learning Management System" like Classes. Course syllabi structure, affirm, and challenge our beliefs about what learning is or should look like. And finally, our academic lives are shaped by the experiences we have with a university's culture of documentation – financial aid forms, registration forms, major course requirement checklists, etc… Higher education is a discourse community that uses writing to make these boundaries seem natural and obvious to us rather than arbitrary and planned. I will then present you with a history of how that term has been thought about in that field before presenting you with an analysis of an example of how to apply it to your own studies while at Pace. The aim of all of this is to present you with the foundational knowledge that writing – like learning to drive, for example – is a social act, one that is shaped by not only your own goals and efforts but by the life of the world in which your writing and communication will circulate.

WHAT IS A DISCOURSE COMMUNITY? UNPACKING THEORY AND HISTORY

The concept of a "discourse community" (DC) has been in circulation throughout the field of rhetoric and writing studies since at least the mid-1980s when applied linguist John Swales heard the term used in a lecture while he was directing the English Language Institute at the University of Michigan (Swales, 2017). But it is important that we first begin by defining the word "discourse." Arguably, the most influential definition of the word ***discourse*** comes from literacy scholar James Paul Gee. Discourse, he wrote in 1989, is "a socially accepted association among ways of using language, of thinking, and of acting, that can be used to identify oneself as a member of a socially meaningful group" (Gee, 1989, p.18). Swales, who had become interested in how academic genres[15] work, theorized that members of academic communities were bound to one another by the reading, writing, and speaking practices they shared in common. Writing in his book Genre Analysis: English in Academic and Research Settings, Swales (1990) defined ***discourse communities*** as "…a group of people who link up in order to pursue goals". Such groups are characterized as:

1. Having a broadly agreed upon set of public goals.
2. Establishing mechanisms of intercommunication among its members.
3. Using participatory mechanisms to provide information and feedback.
4. Utilizing and hence possessing one or more genres in the communicative furtherance of their aims.
5. Acquiring and/or developing a specialized language or "lexis."

---

15 Examples from Swales' work over the years include analysis of "academic" genres like the literature review, grant proposals, research articles, and research presentations.

6. Maintaining a threshold level of members with a suitable level .of context and expertise.

Swales' (1990; 2017) original characteristics in Genre Analysis were published during a period when scholars had been writing for almost a decade in response to the idea of DCs. While Swales (2017) admitted to not having made much of his initial encounter with the term until the late 1980s, by 1986, rhetoric and writing scholars Patricia Bizzell and James E. Porter had taken up the issue. For Bizzell (2003), it was important to emphasize the historical nature of a discourse community, asserting that a DC is not simply "a group who has agreed to abide by certain language rules…[but] an interpretive community whose larger language using habits are part of a larger pattern of regular interaction with the material world" (p. 398). In other words, users of language who are connected to one another, must use writing to make sense of a world that is constantly changing, and that includes rules, regulations, and standards. This makes their use of writing not just an exercise in following genre conventions, but an understanding that rules and standards are historically specific or "situated" rather than universal (Bizzell, 2003, p. 398). In a similar way, Porter wrote (1986) that discourse communities are part of a dynamic that depends on rules and regulations as a way of making decisions about what "approved channels" there will be for members to participate meaningfully in the group. Those channels or "forums," he writes, are also historical in the sense that what counts as acceptable communication can change periodically, as when a new editor takes over at a magazine, newspaper, or academic journal.

What is helpful about Porter's analysis is his emphasis on the relationship texts have to other texts in the context of a discourse community. For instance, he uses the example of publishing a manuscript in the Journal of Applied Psychology, noting that it takes more than following the formatting rules of the APA style guide. A manuscript must engender a sense of trust in its readers. This "ethos" is established by the credibility of the writer, presumably an expert in the area with all of the credentials and affordances that being a recognized expert brings. Then, a manuscript must also demonstrate that it "contributes knowledge" in the form of original research findings; doing so by demonstrating an awareness of previous work [think here of a literature review] in the field and then applying the scientific method to the analysis of research findings in way that is consistent with the community's needs and expectations for "test design", "analysis of results", and "degree of accuracy" (Porter, 1986, p. 40). These characteristics, then, shape the identities and behaviors of aspiring members of the discourse community. To illustrate the complexity of these characteristics, consider my initial story at the beginning of this essay.

CHARACTERISTIC 1

Earlier, I detailed how entering into the community of drivers in my state required a series of steps for the initiation into membership. First, you'll recall, I took a written exam and answered the majority of the questions correctly. I did this by studying a hundred-page driver's manual. After passing the written test, I was issued a temporary driver's license – a learner's permit – which gave me permission to operate the vehicle. The obvious should be noted here – because it will figure into this discussion – that at the time I was issued the permit, I did not know how to operate the vehicle safely. According to Swales' most recent update, DCs have a broadly agreed upon a set of goals, some of which may be argued over between members of the DC (Swales, 2017).

Applying this to my example, the driving community does have an agreed upon set of goals, which is established in the opening pages of the Driver's Manual:

> This manual is designed to help you become a safe driver. It presents many of Pennsylvania's laws governing driving. It should be used as a general guide to the laws but not as a substitute for the Pennsylvania Vehicle Code, which contains the laws affecting Pennsylvania's drivers and vehicles. It should also be noted that the information contained in this manual is subject to change.
>
> The purpose of this manual is to prepare you to take the driver's examination and to obtain a Pennsylvania driver's license. However, the rules of the road and traffic operation principles presented in this manual apply to the three types of vehicles recognized by Pennsylvania law: bicycles, horse-drawn vehicles, and motor vehicles.
>
> If you are learning to drive, this manual will give you all the information you need to study for the driver's examination. If you already have a Pennsylvania driver's license, you can use this manual to review some of the rules of the road you may have forgotten or to learn about some of the rules that may be new or have changed since you received your license. (Bureau of Driver Licensing, 2021, p.i)

This introduction establishes two very important features of DCs. The first is the public nature of the goals that are agreed upon by members of the community. It might be tempting to view "safety" as the goal of the document's stated intention. After all, the entire community depends on these documents and texts to promote safety. However, when we consider the actual sentence, the introduction connects the very idea of safety or that of safe drivers as something that takes becoming. In other words, it's a process that one goes through – from unlicensed (and therefore unsafe) driver to a licensed (and therefore "safe") driver. The second feature is to establish as a goal the notion of membership as a historically situated status. As we saw, there is a process of initiation and a statement that calls on members to remain current by using the manual as a way to "review" and "learn about some of the rules that may have changed" (Bureau of Driver Licensing, 2021, p.1). Regulation, then, is "subject to change" and also requires the active participation of members. Because the regulatory policies and laws that govern driving are the result of state agencies, they are an expression of not only the will of the people, as it were, but also the recognition that such will is contingent and subject to legislation. In that sense, it is more explicitly historical.

CHARACTERISTIC 2

The second characteristic Swales identifies is "mechanisms of intercommunication between members" (Swales, 2017). Swales' initial understanding of this characteristic could not anticipate the proliferation of digital forums that would make it possible for diverse groups of members to participate in the public discussions informing the previously discussed agreed upon goals. For example, the Facebook page for the Pennsylvania Department of Transportation (PennDOT) posts regular articles and informational pieces that can then be commented upon. Consider a recent post by PennDOT. In this announcement, drivers are reminded that the rules for driving include leaving the left lane open for easing the traffic flow. Unlike the driver's manual that is describing driving as a process of going from a novice or beginner to an experienced driver, this post addresses all drivers as though there were no hierarchies of skill. Instead, there is a tone of deference to drivers by asking them to "please" do something so that they can "help." As a public forum for drivers to participate in the conversation, the comment section is insightful as well because of how drivers interact with one another and with the agency. Their resistance to the regulatory language embedded in their post is seen in the defense offered by John Puffmoore who points out that the right lane's overuse is damaging to their car's suspension. Another poster, Don Cooper, reminds Puffmoore that they're breaking the law by driving in the left lane.

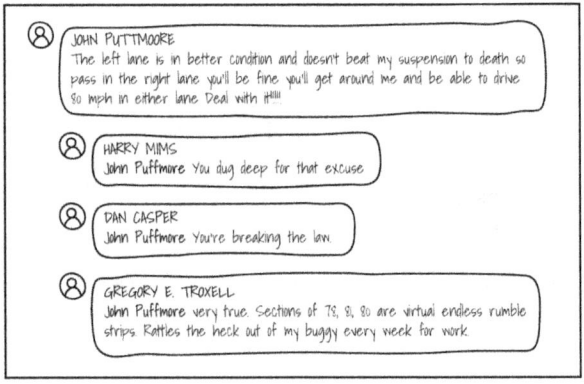

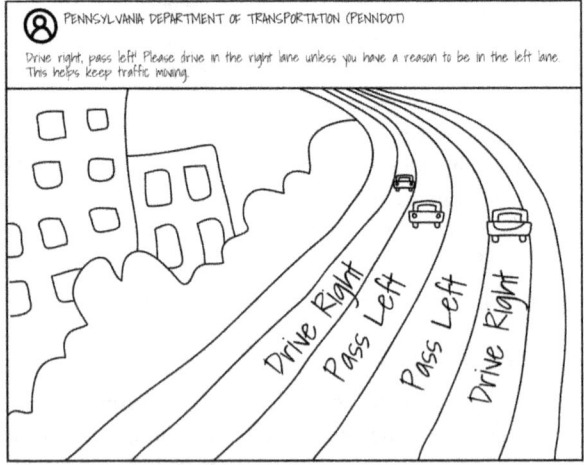

CHARACTERISTIC 3

When it comes to the driving community, we might consider the textual interactions between different groups such as the Pennsylvania Department of Transportation, but we might also consider the larger groups of drivers that exist outside of Pennsylvania. Periodicals like Car and Driver, Popular Mechanics, and BUSRide Magazine all consider different aspects of the driving community. Swales' update also accounts for this development from the original 1990 explanation by noting that discourse communities exist at different levels. Swales identifies what he calls local, focal, and "folocal" discourse communities. Because driving is a membership that exists in different ways across contexts, it is necessary, he writes, to understand they are "differentiated by various factors, such as how localized they are, what origins they have had, and what types of activities are central to their existence" (Swales, 2017). For drivers, *local discourse communities* would certainly involve agencies that speak to the regional and/or provincial needs and expectations of a membership – for example, PennDOT in Pennsylvania or, in New York, it might be the New York State Department of Motor Vehicles. But even within those local agencies, there are branch offices that, while subject to state regulations, will also have their own local policies and procedures. The most common of these are the hours of operation that can be different from one county to the next.

Focal discourse communities, on the other hand, have a broader reach and can speak to parts of the driving community that have a variety of interests but that somehow transcend regional interest (Swales, 2017). Chauffeur Driven, for example, is a trade magazine for the limousine and luxury ground transportation industry. The magazine features profiles of industry leaders and feature stories on the training of CEOs in the industry. *"Folocal" discourse communities,* on the other hand, "are hybrid communities whose members have a double—and sometimes split—allegiance, as they are confronted by internal and external challenges and pressures" (Swales, 2017). If you have ever heard an advertisement talking about "your local Chevy dealer," this is what they're talking about. It is this sense that communities of drivers can be bound by driving the same kind of car. This is seen whenever there is a recall by the manufacturer for a specific car. The issues that affect drivers of a Chevy TrailBlazer in Burlington, Vermont will be identical to those in Pleasantville, NY when there is a factory recall.

CHARACTERISTIC 4

The fourth characteristic Swales identifies is the circulation of genres that bind members of discourse communities to one another. We might consider in my example how this can be complicated when it comes to thinking about the genres of communication that link drivers to one other in any state and beyond, given the intricacies of membership. It is helpful, first, to return to Gee's understanding of discourse because, as he points out, the uses of language – that is, the examples of reading, speaking, and writing that form a community's practices – are an "identity toolkit which comes complete with the appropriate costume and instructions on how to act and talk, so as to take on a particular role that others will recognize" (Gee, 1989, p.18). As students, we all learn about the relationship between genres, such as the multiple choice question quiz, the term paper, the book report, or the science project, and our understanding of what learning is. We internalize this relationship with genres that help to solidify this connection; think of the report card, for example. These uses of language naturalize or make invisible the connection we make between being a student and being quizzed on the lesson. Genres help to perform this socialization into an identity by masking the relations of power that are established through one's participation.

Let's look at being a licensed driver to see how this works.

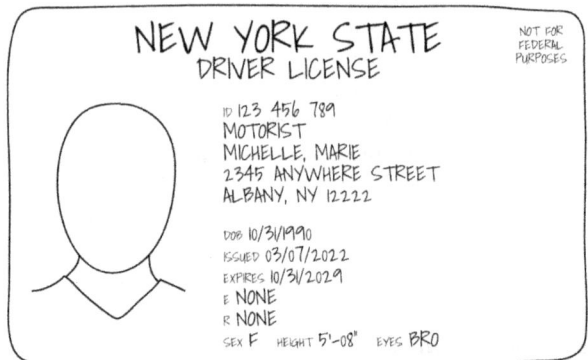

A common genre that illustrates the way texts help to construct our identities as members of a discourse community is the driver's license itself. It is a document that functions in so many situations as one's primary means of identification. In New York State, for example, a license includes as a background a faded image of the Seal of the State of New York, an image of the driver, their current address, and dates of birth/license validation. Physical characteristics like height and eye color also appear on the text. What is tricky here is that the genre does not speak to the driver's ability. For example, it doesn't list the score of the written exam or the road test. Instead, the generic conventions of the driver's license tacitly assert (and by default our participation legitimizes this) that our identity as members of a discourse community is the consequence of the state's endorsement. In other words, only the state can say whether or not the driver is permitted to operate a motor vehicle. But as the genre makes clear, ability and permission have little to do with one another when one needs to use the document. Surrendering the document to a traffic officer, presenting it to the FedEx office to pick up a package, or using it to purchase alcohol, are common, experiences that illustrate the genre's use in other discourse communities. .

CHARACTERISTIC 5

Swales' fifth characteristic involves the discourse community's use of a specialized language or "lexis" (Swales, 2017). A "folocal" discourse community, such as owners of a 2022 Ford Escape, might experience membership in the discourse community of drivers through their vehicle, the way smartphone users organize themselves around whether or not they use an iPhone or an Android phone. In the owner's manual, for example, there is a glossary of symbols that may appear on the dashboard of the car. These symbols familiarize drivers with a way of reading their dashboard so that they can make decisions about how to operate their vehicle or when to have it serviced.

A specialized vocabulary that is more conventional is also a part of membership in the community. Two classes of vocabulary illustrate the complexity of this characteristic. The first is vocabulary that is acquired through the act of driving. Knowing that a speedometer measures how fast one is traveling is something that a driver learns by operating a vehicle.

- Engine oil
- Fan warning
- Flammable
- Fuel pump reset
- Hazard flashers
- Headlamps on
- Hill descent control
- Interior luggage compartment release
- Keep out of reach of children
- Low fuel level
- Maintain correct fluid level
- Note operating instructions
- Parking aid
- Passenger airbag activated

Similarly, the odometer measures how many miles a vehicle has traveled. The second class of vocabulary is one that is learned through direct instruction. For example, you can't learn about the catalytic converter from driving a car. The 2022 Ford Escape Owner's Manual explains, for example, that the catalytic converter "is part of your vehicle's emissions system which filters harmful pollutants from the exhaust gas" (Ford Motor Company, 2022). In turn, this requires some basic knowledge by the driver/owner of the vehicle to know that an internal combustion engine will emit toxic exhaust gas as a byproduct of burning fuel. These two classes of specialized vocabulary illustrate the complexity of a discourse community such as that of drivers.

The literacy represented here goes far beyond the ability to read and write, but instead, how these practices are socially sanctioned activities, that is, they are sponsored by the community at large in two ways: acquisition and learning. For Gee, literacy acquisition – and therefore, control over a discourse – happens through "exposure to models, and a process of trial and error, without a process of formal instruction" (Gee, 1989, p. 18). Additionally, he writes, "it happens in natural settings which are meaningful and functional in the sense that the acquirer knows that he needs to acquire the thing he is exposed to in order to function and the acquirer in fact wants to function" (Gee, 1989, p. 18). Gee contrasts this to learning which "is a process that involves conscious knowledge gained through teaching…[which] involves explanation and analysis." (Gee, 1989, p. 18). In my case, I experienced both of these encounters with specialized language when I had to make sense of a work report of what was done to my car when the engine suddenly began to stall when I would stop at a traffic light. This is how I learned what an Exhaust Gas Recirculation (EGR) valve was.

CHARACTERISTIC 6

Maintaining a threshold level of members is Swales' sixth characteristic. This one is the least complicated for my example because anyone associated with the act of driving can be said to be a member of the discourse community – this includes anyone with a driver's license or any focal/local discourse community that is organized around driving – mechanics of special types of cars, car dealerships, driver education instructors, and traffic officers just to name a few.

CONCLUSION

On the day I sat down to write this conclusion, I walked down the street to my car and began a lengthy commute to work. I remember feeling pretty excited about the day, especially since it was a bright and sunny one. I was feeling confident about what I was going to teach in class and I was looking forward to seeing my students. About a mile into my drive, just before taking the onramp to one of the busiest parkways in New York City, a sensation of worry came over me. It was a feeling of disconnection, of feeling like I did not belong. I felt worried and anxious. I realized I had left my driver's license in my apartment. All of a sudden every traffic light, every turn, every encounter with an erratic driver was the potential to be found out and perhaps ticketed or even jailed, who knows, I thought. After I picked up my license and felt back to normal, I thought about what I had felt and how much, was invested in this document. Somehow, possession of this text gave me security about my relationship to my abilities and how they might be perceived if I were to get in an accident or break a rule.

I think when we go to college, we enter into a similar kind of relationship. Discourse communities, which we experience as "majors" that are offered by "departments," are animated by the social world of the university, which is its own discourse community. Like a driver, or "motorist", the process of becoming a member is one of socialization, where we learn to internalize and self-police our behaviors. When I forgot my driver's license and realized I was operating a vehicle, that little feeling inside was oh no I'm a criminal. It's not an accident to have felt that way. The genres of that discourse community taught me what the relationship was between my ability to drive a car and the institutions that regulate its practice – in other words, my relationship to the state.

All kinds of texts circulate within our discourse communities (business, economics, criminal justice, psychology, etc...) to socialize us into an understanding of the university as a culture of endorsement and sponsorship. This exists in genres like the letter of recommendation or written commentary on one's work. These systems of certification also work to legalize or "sanction" our learning as a process that is sponsored by an institution. The genre of the Identification Card works in this way. A student is no less a learner, no less intelligent, or capable of doing academic work because they don't have an ID card. Understanding discourse communities and the six characteristics Swales offers, is to understand the difference between being a student and being a learner. Our discourse communities are structured to socialize our identities so that the culture of endorsement and sponsorship which is supported by systems of certification that centralize authority and power among those who are credentialed (professors, deans, etc..). The question before us, then, is almost always the same. How can we balance our need to cultivate our own learning and growth with our need to be recognized and certified by an institution?

While this question is generally experienced as a philosophical one, it is worth thinking about it in practical terms because it is always part of the social context of a university. There, the drama of becoming someone new happens at the same time we are learning about who we have been. This realization can create an unstable experience as you learn to gain control over your language in writing situations that call you to recognize different parts of yourself. For example, a literacy narrative is a common genre in first-year writing. It typically asks you to both tell a story about your history with reading and writing while also reflecting and analyzing its meaning. An assignment like this often asks you to assume the role of narrator or storyteller, where experiences are recalled as discrete moments that are exemplary. It makes sense, then, that you would need to tell that story from the perspective of the first person, where the pronoun "I" would be appropriate. On the other hand, literacy narratives also have an analytical component, where the narrator also reflects and draws conclusions about an abstract concept like literacy. Because we often internalize "rules" like "never use the first person pronoun in academic writing," we sometimes don't know what to do in a moment where we need to draw some kind of abstract conclusion about reading and writing. School trains all of us to detach our lived experiences from the processes of reflection, analysis, and argument – conventional features of the university-as-discourse community. This can leave us – I know it has for me – uncertain about how to connect our lives to the subjects we study. The trick, if there is one, is not to confuse that really important question with its symptom: the writer's decision about using "I" in a paper. What all of us – students, teachers, administrators – ought to remember is that universities are discourse communities because they are made up of people. And because they are made up of people, that means they are made up of values, assumptions, and beliefs that are always subject to change. As you explore what it means to be a writer, you will learn that the answer to a question like that will change depending on where you are asking it. If it gets especially tough, just remember that it's easier than trying to figure out what it means to be a good driver.

DISCUSSION QUESTIONS AND ACTIVITIES

1. Compile a list of genres that you might find in your first-year writing course, such as the syllabus and assignments. What kinds of DCs – local, focal, folocal – can you identify in these documents?
2. How and where do you see the characteristics Swales offers in these genres?
3. How do they demonstrate the university as a culture of endorsement and sponsorship?
4. How do they support the systems of certification that help people become socialized into their discourse communities?
5. In what ways might these documents challenge what is understood as the characteristics of a university and/or a DC like rhetoric and writing studies?

REFERENCES

Bizzell, P. (2003). Cognition, convention, and certainty: what we need to know about writing. In Victor Villanueva (Ed.), Cross talk in comp theory: a reader (pp. 387-412). NCTE.

Gee, J. P. (1989). What is literacy? Journal of Education, 171(1), pp. 18-23. https://doi.org/10.1177/002205748917100102

Porter, J. E. (1986). Intertextuality and the discourse community. Rhetoric Review, 5(1), pp. 34-47.

Swales, J. M. (1990). Genre analysis: English in academic and research settings. Cambridge UP.

Swales, J. M. (2017). The concept of discourse community: some recent personal history. Composition Forum, 37. https://compositionforum.com/issue/37/swales-retrospective.php

CHAPTER 3

FORGING A WRITING PROCESS

Christina Gonzalez

CHAPTER OUTCOMES

- Recognize writing as a social act.
- Explain aspects of process writing.
- Develop an approach to the writing process.

KEY TERMS

- Writing Process
- Collaborative Writing
- Writing Community
- Higher Order Concerns
- Lower Order Concerns
- Audience

CHAPTER OVERVIEW

This chapter situates you within the context of writing, examines writing processes and applications, and addresses writing as a social act that requires collaboration and support. The writing to follow draws attention to the process nature of the course, an approach to writing practice and instruction that calls for students to generate ideas, complete multiple drafts, reflect on their writing, and conference with their peers and instructor, respectively.

WRITING IS A PROCESS

In this class, writing is a process of creativity, reflection, and critique that is valued more than the final product (Murray, 2024; Elbow, 1998). This process supports you and your classmates to develop an understanding of how and why you write in particular contexts and genres. Process writing is recursive and iterative, meaning that writing steps are revisited over multiple drafts (Lacy & Gagich, 2017; Seow, 2002). For example, brainstorming happens throughout an assignment, not only in the early stage. While process is really *processes*, in the sense that how we go about writing varies from person to person, in the early stage of your writing development, we will follow a scaffolded version of the writing process for all three projects:

Introduction to Genre ⟹ idea generation and pre-drafting activities ⟹ draft 1 and writer's notes ⟹ instructor feedback conference and revision plan ⟹ draft 2 and writer's notes ⟹ peer feedback workshop and revision plan ⟹ final draft and project reflection.

MESSY FIRST DRAFTS

The first step of the writing process is *pre-writing*, a generative phase where you will develop your purpose, identify your audience, and begin to create new ideas (DeJoy, 1998). After reviewing the assignment, understanding its specific parameters and expectations, and determining the audience, it's time to get started (Lacy & Gagich, 2017). Of course, if you are unsure what the assignment is asking of you, please consult with your instructor or make an appointment at the writing center. With the assignment clear, you will begin generating ideas, conducting preliminary research, and/or reviewing sample texts. Some additional practices to get you started include list-making, outlining, and freewriting. The goal is to allow yourself to be uncensored and unrestricted. Don't worry about organization, structure, grammar, spelling, or punctuation; just write (Elbow, 1998). These exercises will help you find clarity and direction in your writing and may conclude with a research question, thesis statement, or controlling idea. As noted above, what you decide early in your writing may change as you grow to better understand your selected topic and the genre you compose (Lacy & Gagich, 2017). In the prewriting stage, you may find it helpful to gain feedback. We suggest checking in with a friend, talking with a classmate, meeting with your instructor, or making an appointment at the writing center. Remember, getting feedback or brainstorming does not and should not happen just once; rather, it should occur in any and all stages of writing.

After completing some pre-writing, you will write your *messy* first draft. This is only your first attempt; go easy on yourself and know that first drafts, as Lamott (2005) so eloquently stated, are often *shitty*. With the draft in hand, you will next engage with your peers and instructor–the members of your classroom writing community. In one-on-one conferences and peer workshops, you will focus on higher-order writing concerns (HOC), such as meeting the assignment expectations, developing a clear and critical purpose, and logically organizing your thoughts for an audience. When revising a first draft, you are doing the arduous work of moving paragraphs, expanding ideas, cutting unnecessary language, and working to bring focus to your text and audience. To be clear, this is not a Grammarly exercise in which you delegate your writing responsibilities to a software program that addresses sentence-level concerns, such as grammar, spelling, and punctuation. These changes take place later in the writing process. Early feedback interactions with your peers and instructor are designed to address one or two areas for improvement toward your controlling purpose. Unlike many of your past experiences, you are not expected to point out and correct every error. There are no red pens in this class. The writing center is also available to provide additional feedback, bring clarity to the feedback you received, or help begin the revision process.

A SOCIAL AND COLLABORATIVE ACT

Writing is a social and collaborative act that will move, guide, and support you through each stage of writing (DeJoy, 2004; Elbow, 1998). As you may have noticed, this class values interaction between students and faculty. In the earliest writing stage, we talk with people to help shape our nascent thoughts into something more substantive. Revising is an act of communication, moments when you engage with your audience and determine where you are successfully and unsuccessfully meeting their needs and expectations (Pratt, 1999), what Lamott (2005) called *times of trial and error*. Through the feedback we receive from our peers and instructors, we revise according to audience reception and understanding. Writing requires the exchange of ideas–a process of give and take between the writer and their audience (Elbow, 1998). When partaking in and contributing to these conversations, your thoughts evolve (Pratt, 1999). Taking action during these moments of transition will help you create more sophisticated writing as you learn how others perceive your work. Engaging with your writing community allows you the time and space to consider your choices and how to move and revise for future drafts. Collaboration is difficult work that requires all members of the class to willingly and actively engage with each other and their drafts.

REFLECTING THROUGHOUT

To improve as a writer, students must become reflective thinkers. As writers, we are always reflecting in one way or another: thinking back on what we have written, considering what was discussed in conferences and workshops, and determining if we have met our own and others' expectations. In this class, reflection can take on many forms, such as short in-class reflections, journal reflections that accompany your drafts, and robust reflections that occur at the end of the unit and semester. Reflective writing within the writing process is an opportunity for you to evaluate the feedback received and determine the next logical steps considering the state of your draft, and your purpose, audience, and assignment criteria. Reflective writing allows you to highlight the skills you have learned or applied and calls for you to think about how they can transfer to other writing or communication contexts. Reflection is, at times, a counterintuitive practice, as the act of looking back is what propels you forward.

THE RECURSIVE PROCESS OF REVISION

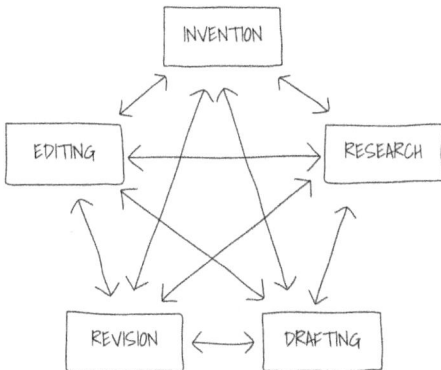

When moving from one draft to the next, you will apply instructor, peer, and writing consultant feedback, as well as your critical assessment of your work. Following the process mapped out above, after revising, you will return to conferences and workshops. This again reminds us that writing is recursive (Lacy & Gagich, 2017; Seow, 2002). In workshops, you may brainstorm new ways to address an issue you are facing or possibly create an outline to better organize the sequence of your ideas and paragraphs. Once you have determined your writing meets the assignment's expectations, has a critical purpose, and is effectively organized, you may consider your use of source material, ability to synthesize and analyze information, sequence of ideas, and continuity between thoughts, sentences, and paragraphs. These, too, are higher-order concerns, which we could call a second tier. Once the higher-order concerns are addressed, you may turn to a lower-order concern. Lower-order concerns focus on sentence-level issues, such as sentence structure or word choice, to name a few. Reflection proceeds and follows all drafts just as you did in the first.

CONCLUSION

Writing is a process of recursively assessing, revising, reflecting, and editing that takes place in and among a community of writers. While this practice is presented and honed in your writing classes, it is relevant to the work you will do across academic disciplines and professional fields. This, as discussed earlier, is known as writing transfer, a product of reflection that moves writing knowledge from one context and applies it to others. Writing as a process is designed to help you become a better, more confident writer. It provides you an approach to address assignments and language to navigate writing and revision. Good writing does not just happen when you put words down on the page in hopes of addressing assignment expectations. Instead, it occurs only through time and effort, a dedication to yourself and your class community (DeJoy, 2004; Elbow, 1998).

DISCUSSION QUESTIONS AND ACTIVITIES

1. What has been your writing process before coming to this class?
2. How do you determine what changes to make between drafts?
3. What role has communication with peers and teachers played in your previous writing?
4. How can your peers and instructor support you through the writing process?
5. How do you believe you may support your peers?

REFERENCES

Barila, B. (2016). Integrating mindfulness into anti-oppression pedagogy. Routledge.
DeJoy, N. (2004). Undergraduate writing in composition studies. Utah State University Press.
Elbow, P. (1998). Writing with power. Oxford University Press.
Lacy, S., & Gagich, E. (2017). The Writing Process, Composing, and Revising. A Guide to Rhetoric, Genre, and Success in First-Year Writing. Pressbooks.
Lamott, A. (2005). Shitty first drafts. In P. Eschholz, A. Rosa, & V. Clark (Eds.), *Language awareness: Readings for college writers* (pp. 93-96). Boston: Bedford/St. Martin.
Murray, D. M. (2024). Teach Writing as a Process Not Product. In K.L. Arola & V. Villanueva (Eds). *Cross-Talk in Comp Theory*. NCTE.
Pratt, M. L. (1999). Ways of Reading (5th edition). In D. Bartholomae & A. Petroksky (Eds.). Arts of the contact zone. New York: Bedford/St. Martin's.
Seow, A. (2002). The Writing Process and Process Writing. In J. C. Richards & W. A. Renandya (Eds.), Methodology in Language Teaching: An Anthology of Current Practice (pp. 315–320). Cambridge: Cambridge University Press.

CHAPTER 4

TOWARD AN UNDERSTANDING OF WRITING AND RHETORIC

Katherine Dye

CHAPTER OUTCOMES
- Define rhetoric and explain its role in communication and persuasion.
- Discuss how shifts in the rhetorical situation might change the message or the way it is delivered.
- Apply rhetorical appeals and strategies to written text and images.

KEY TERMS
- Rhetoric
- Rhetorical Situation
- Ethos
- Pathos
- Logos
- Kairos

CHAPTER OVERVIEW

In this chapter, you will learn about rhetoric, how it works, and why it is vital for your college career and beyond. It will also explore how to use rhetoric in your writing and communication inside and outside the classroom.

DEFINING RHETORIC

Aristotle (1994), the ancient Greek philosopher and one of the foundational figures in our understanding of rhetoric, writes in his text called, appropriately enough, *On Rhetoric* that rhetoric is "the faculty of observing in any given case the available means of persuasion" (p. 7). This itself is not a bad definition, though it might be a bit misleading. Rhetoric and persuasion are often seen as almost interchangeable, and while rhetoric might be used as a *means* of persuasion, this is not rhetoric's sole function. And, to make things even more complicated, while typically understood as something associated with words, speech, and writing, rhetoric can just as easily refer to the nonverbal: images, gestures, and sounds. Understanding that rhetoric is not only limited to text and speech, we should consider Duffy's (2023) contention that "Whether we understand rhetoric as persuasion, effective communication, or social action, practically every human behavior can be understood as rhetoric" (p. 259 In short, as Duffy has argued, "Rhetoric is everything and everything is rhetoric" (p. 259).

CONSIDERING THE RHETORICAL SITUATION

Rhetoric doesn't happen in a vacuum; it happens in context with purpose. This is called the rhetorical situation. According to Bitzer (1968), the "rhetorical situation" is essentially the context for a rhetorical action, which can include the "persons, events, objects [and] relations" involved in the situation along with a demand or "exigence" for rhetorical action (p. 5). In slightly simpler terms, the rhetorical situation is "any set of circumstances that involves at least one person using some sort of communication to modify the perspective of at least one other person" (Purdue Owl, n.d.). In this moment, a *writer* engages with an *audience* in a specific *setting* at a precise *time* with a distinct *purpose* to address a defined *problem*, known as *exigence*.

Figure 1:

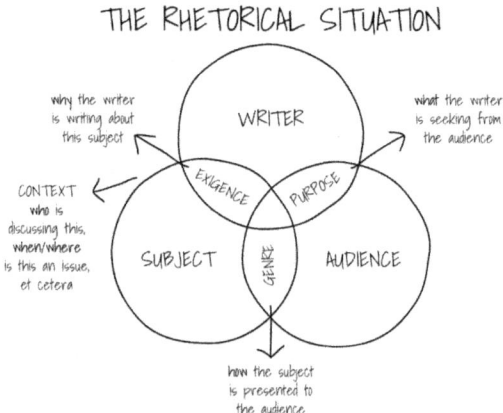

RHETORICAL APPEALS

Once the rhetorical situation has been established, you must then decide which rhetorical appeals you believe are appropriate to the situation. A rhetorical appeal is a method or approach by which an author or speaker attempts to evoke the reaction they want in an audience. There are traditionally four different types of rhetorical appeals, which were themselves initially defined by Aristotle.

Ethos refers to any argument that makes an appeal to either authorial credibility or an audience's values. When appealing to authorial credibility, the author attempts to prove their own knowledge or qualifications for discussing the subject at hand. In order to evoke authorial credibility, an author might cite their experience and specific qualifications. When appealing to an audience's values, an author might make reference to common ground, such as shared ideology or values. In this sense, the author will appeal to the audience's sense of morality and "rightness" (Gagich & Zickel, Ethos: Appeal to Values/Trust).

Pathos refers to any argument that appeals to the audience's emotions. An argument using Pathos will try to evoke an emotion in the audience in order to make its point or to persuade. This will serve to make the audience more "open" and to feel more connected to the author. The emotions evoked can be anything from fury to sadness to desire to joy to disgust, as it is entirely up to the author to decide which emotion would be the most useful to them in their particular rhetorical situation. Some specific ways an author might employ Pathos are through the use of expressive language, vivid imagery, and the sharing of particularly resonant stories or anecdotes (Gagich & Zickel, Pathos: Appeal to Emotions).

Logos refers to any argument that makes an appeal to logic and rationality. With Logos, an author is trying to appeal to an audience's intellect by presenting organized, thorough, well-sequenced, logical arguments that are ostensibly free of bias. An argument employing Logos might also bring in known facts, numbers, and statistics to make its point. It also uses logical comparisons, deductive and inductive reasoning, clear examples, and cause/effect thinking (Gagich & Zickel, Logos: Appeal to Logic).

The last rhetorical appeal, *Kairos*, is often less discussed in writing. It refers to precise timing or finding the opportune moment to perform a rhetorical action. It refers to the fact that finding the correct moment to present rhetoric can have an enormous effect on how an audience receives it (Cronkhite, 7.1 Overview of Kairos).

RHETORICAL ANALYSIS OF I HAVE A DREAM

To better understand rhetoric, we will now consider its application by reviewing an excerpt of Dr. Martin Luther King, Jr.'s famous "I Have a Dream" speech, which he delivered on the steps of the Lincoln Memorial in Washington, D.C., on August 28, 1963, during the March on Washington for Jobs and Freedom. This event marked a pivotal moment in the civil rights movement, and King's speech is one of the main elements that we still remember decades later. It has become a key reference point for activists, politicians, historians, and the general public ever since.

> I have a dream that one day, down in Alabama, with its vicious racists, with its governor having his lips dripping with the words of "interposition" and "nullification"-- one day right there in Alabama little black boys and black girls will be able to join hands with little white boys and white girls as sisters and brothers.

> I have a *dream* today!

> I have a dream that one day every valley shall be exalted, and every hill and mountain shall be made low, the rough places will be made plain, and the crooked places will be made straight; and the glory of the Lord shall be revealed and all flesh shall see it together.

> This is our hope, and this is the faith that I go back to the South with. (King, 2010)

Dr. King masterfully sets up his *rhetorical situation*. He engages with an *audience* (his fellow participants in the March on Washington as well as, in a wider sense, all Americans) within the *context* of the Civil Rights movement on the steps of the Lincoln Memorial in Washington D.C. (Washington D.C. being the nation's capital and Abraham Lincoln being the US president to issue the Emancipation Proclamation during the Civil War in 1863, freeing all slaves in the United States) during the March on Washington in 1963 (one hundred years after the Emancipation Proclamation was issued) his ***purpose*** being to provide encouragement and inspiration to address the ***exigence*** of continued racial segregation in America.

In this speech, King uses his talent as a writer and speaker and his command of rhetoric to share his vision of the United States as one free of segregation, prejudice, and racism. He applies rhetoric to build solidarity by defining a racially diverse social group to combat segregation ("little black boys and black girls will be able to join hands with little white boys and white girls as sisters and brothers"), constructing meanings and identities (the characterization of "vicious racists" in Alabama, including the governor), coordinating behavior, mediating power, and attempting to produce social change (the emphasis on collective action). Furthermore, King employs *anaphora*, the repetition of a word or phrase, by underscoring his "dream" for racial reconciliation.

In terms of rhetorical appeals, King makes particular use of ***Ethos*** and ***Pathos***. In terms of Ethos, his role as a Baptist pastor affords him credibility as a speaker in that his dream is divinely righteous. His language calls for *collective* action. King makes use of Ethos to appeal to his audience not only by emphasizing collective responsibility and values ("This is our hope") but he also makes biblical references, which serve to underscore the religious underpinnings of his mission ("and the glory of the Lord shall be revealed and all flesh shall see it together.") In terms of Pathos, King uses powerful language and imagery both to condemn his opponents ("Alabama, with its vicious racists") and to evoke the harmonious future he envisions ("little black boys and black girls will be able to join hands with little white boys and white girls as sisters and brothers.") Throughout his entire speech, King makes use of a wide variety of rhetorical tools to articulate his arguments, and this effectiveness can be attested to by the speech's undeniable historical significance.

RHETORIC, CULTURE, AND IDENTITY

While rhetoric can be used as a force for change, rhetoric also always exists inside a wider culture that determines aspects of how it is created and received. This brings us to the question: When someone says the word "culture" to you, what do you think of? You may think about the culture of a specific country, referring to its language, traditions, behaviors, practices, or food, or you may think of "culture" in terms of the arts, like painting, sculpture, photography, music, dance, theater, and film. In the social sciences, one potential definition that has been put forward is that rather than being a set of "things," culture is a set of "practices." Stuart Hall (1997) stated that culture is defined by the exchange of meanings between individuals in a society or group. Culture, therefore, is primarily a means of making sense of the world.

This definition significantly opens up the idea of "culture" as a concept. And if we extrapolate a little further, we can see that it is through "culture" that we create meaning in our world: "It is participants in a culture who give meaning to people, objects, and events. Things 'in themselves' rarely if ever have any one, single, fixed and unchanging meaning" (Hall, 1997). If culture refers to specific practices rather than to specific "things" and culture creates meaning, then this suggests that through our own engagement in making meaning, we create culture.

If we create culture, then we also situate ourselves within that culture, and this is where we come to the production of identity. Our identities are constructed by our relationships to the people, places, and things that exist around us. Braxton McNulty (2021) stated:

> [...] identity has quite a broad definition, but it is severely influenced by the setting the word is looked at in along with how one perceives the idea. The places people go and the groups people surround themselves with are the ones who directly impact an individual's identity. Furthermore, a person's identity can be shaped by the words they hear, and the fact that not everybody is going to interpret them in the same way is why rhetoric is needed. (para. 8)

Rhetoric comes into play with culture and identity when we consider the practice of cultural rhetorics, which entails "be[ing] willing to build meaningful theoretical frames from inside the particular culture in which you are situating [your] work. To do so means understanding a specific culture's systems, beliefs, relationships to the past, practices of meaning-making, and practices of carrying culture forward to future generations" (Bratta & Powell, 2016, para. 8). Cultural rhetorics are, therefore, the practice of identifying and understanding the processes of meaning-making in a given culture. As a result, culture, identity, and rhetoric are entirely interconnected. Rhetoric provides you the tools to make sense of your relationship to your own culture and identity as well as to understand how different groups and identities relate to each other.

RHETORIC THAT SHAPES AMERICA

The Statue of Liberty

Let's look at an example of a cultural artifact that you are probably familiar with in order to demonstrate this link between culture, identity, and rhetoric. You have almost certainly seen this statue before, perhaps in real life, perhaps in photographs, perhaps even as a keychain in a souvenir shop. What ideas or concepts do you associate with it? Do you feel any kind of personal connection with it, as an American or a New Yorker, or perhaps through some other aspect of your identity? Or do you not feel any connection to it at all? *The Statue of Liberty* can represent (and has represented!) any number of concepts, such as "America," "New York City," "French-American relations," "freedom," "democracy," "strength," "4th of July," "patriotism," and many, many more depending on the context or rhetorical situation in which it is being used. The statue itself, which stands in New York Harbor near Ellis Island, historically served as a symbol to immigrants coming to the United States by ship during the late 19th and early 20th Centuries that they had finally arrived and were on the brink of starting a new life.

Even the location of the statue, on an island in the middle of a busy harbor, serves to amplify its rhetorical power as a symbol of freedom and hope but also of strength and prosperity.

With all that being said, how did this statue come to represent so many things to so many different people? Even disregarding the history and context of the Statue of Liberty, how did this image of a woman with a crown on her head carrying a torch, or to be even more literal, how did this enormous hunk of metal come to represent such varied concepts as "strength," "New York City," "America," and "patriotism"? We can consider the historical context and the fact that, from its very creation, the statue has been featured on merchandise and memorabilia, as well as potent political imagery. It has been featured on posters and pamphlets but also on plates, lamps, quilts, and even pocket knives ("Popular and Commercial Culture," 2018). As a result, with the image distributed far and wide in many different contexts, it has acquired many different meanings and associations that are constantly evolving. This brings us back to Duffy's (2023) assertion that any human behavior (or creation) that seeks to persuade, effectively communicate, or bring about social action can be seen as rhetoric.

World War I Poster
(Sackett & Wilhelms Corp N.Y., 1917)

We can see an example of the Statue of Liberty being used as visual rhetoric in the image above. The ***rhetorical situation*** is as follows: This is a poster from 1917 when the United States government was attempting to raise money for its involvement in World War I. In order to do this, one strategy of the US Treasury and the Federal Reserve was to launch a campaign to encourage Americans to buy war bonds or "Liberty Bonds" as they were called (Sutch, 2015). Part of this effort was to convince Americans that buying these bonds was a patriotic service or duty during wartime, and various forms of rhetoric, visual and otherwise, were employed to accomplish this task. The Statue of Liberty, as seen above, appeared frequently in this rhetoric as a symbol of American liberties and freedoms and was thus used to stir up feelings of loyalty and patriotism in Americans. In the image, the Statue is explicitly aligned with this rhetoric. The image is a poster depicting people who are presumably immigrants coming into New York Harbor aboard a ship and getting their first glimpse of the Statue. It occupies the foreground of the poster and along the top are the words: "Remember Your First Thrill of American Liberty."

The primary rhetorical appeals being used here are: **Ethos** and **Pathos**. In this case, the appeal to **Ethos** is present in the invoking of values such as "American Liberty" and also the words "Your Duty" as these are both related to ideological and ethical values. **Pathos** is invoked by the hopeful image of the passengers on the ship seeing the Statue of Liberty for the first time as well as the direct call to memory and emotion of the words: "Remember Your First Thrill of American Liberty." The image of the Statue of Liberty has the rhetorical power it does because of the place it occupies in American culture and what it means to the individuals who make up that culture. And it is through rhetoric that these meanings are put to work.

RHETORIC OF SOCIAL MEDIA

Though often unnoticed, we engage with rhetorical appeals every single day. Nowhere is this clearer than on social media. For example, an infographic you encounter on Instagram that makes use of (properly sourced) facts and statistics to spread awareness of a political issue might rely on **Logos** to persuade you to recognize and support a cause. Someone recounting a painful experience of being discriminated against in a TikTok or YouTube video might employ **Pathos** to garner support from their viewers. When influencers on social media take sponsorships and advertise different companies' products to their followers, they are employing **Ethos** since they are using their credibility in the eyes of their audience to convince them to buy a product. And **Kairos** can always be a factor, depending on when a particular post might show up in your feed. Once you learn to recognize these rhetorical appeals, you will start to see them everywhere.

Rhetoric, of course, is not limited to political concerns. In the age of 24-hour news coverage and endless threads of social media content, *rhetoric* is all around us. If you have ever witnessed some kind of argument, political or otherwise, in a Twitter thread (or have even been involved in one yourself), you have engaged in or have been subject to rhetoric in some way. And indeed, rhetoric is not only something you have almost certainly been exposed to, but it is also something that you have utilized yourself without even knowing it. If you have ever debated someone, tried to make an argument, expressed a personal opinion, or have engaged in communication in order to bring about a desired effect in the world, you have employed rhetoric in some capacity.

MEME RHETORIC

To give an example, one variety of rhetoric that we often overlook is internet memes. Yes, it might sound silly, but in fact, internet memes are some of the most widely employed rhetorical artifacts today.

Let's look at a template of one as well as an example:

You may have seen this particular meme before in different forms. Figure 5 features a screenshot from Senator Bernie Sanders' December 2019 fundraising video posted to social media for his campaign to become the Democratic Party's 2020 Presidential nominee. The image features Sanders wearing a parka in what appears to be a snowy suburban neighborhood, and the closed captions along the bottom of the image read: "I am once again asking for your financial support." In its original context, this image/video was indeed itself a rhetorical artifact, the *author* being Sanders and his campaign media team, the *audience* being Sanders' supporters and potential donors, the *setting* being the run-up to the 2020 Democratic Primaries and also the setting in the video, where he is in a very typical-looking suburban neighborhood, emphasizing how he values average, working Americans. The *purpose* is to raise money for his campaign, the *text* is a video posted to social media, and finally, the *exigence* is the campaign's need for donations.

Figure 6 shows an example of this image as a meme. The same screenshot of Sanders is used, but above the image, there is text that says: "College kids calling home for the first time in 3 months."

As a meme, the *rhetorical situation* of the image changes, but certain elements remain the same. The *"exigence"* in all forms of this meme is the author or whoever is being presented as the subject of the meme's need or desire for money (usually with a joking or ironic undertone); however, the *author, audience, setting, and purpose* are all variables. While the "content" of the meme and the message will shift depending on who has "created" it and for what purpose, most people who are familiar with this meme will immediately understand the kind of rhetorical situation being evoked when they see it, regardless of the context. This also goes to show how the *rhetorical situation* of the original image/artifact (the screenshot of the campaign video) goes on to inform how the meme is used, and part of the humor of it has to do with the audience's understanding of who Sanders is and the serious rhetorical situation present in the initial image being put in increasingly ridiculous contexts. Rhetoric is not just a serious, stuffy academic topic. It is highly relevant to how we communicate today, and furthermore, effective rhetoric is often characterized by its adaptability, fluidity, and ability to reflect how we see the world around us.

CONCLUSION

Rhetoric can be a deceptively complex topic, and its definition has been a consistently evolving one for thousands of years. It both determines and is determined by culture and identity, and as such, it has paramount importance in how we see each other and the world. However, even if we have difficulty defining it, we can easily recognize it and how it works once we know what to look for. Through understanding the given *rhetorical situation* and all of its constituent parts, as well as the *rhetorical appeals* that are available to us, we can utilize these different tools to speak and write powerfully and effectively in any context.

DISCUSSION QUESTIONS AND ACTIVITIES

1. Before reading this chapter, what did you think rhetoric was? How has your understanding of it changed?
2. When and how have you effectively used rhetoric in recent academic writing?
3. When and how have you effectively used rhetoric in your personal life?
4. Select a meme and describe the rhetorical situation and explain the rhetorical strategies used to convey its message.
5. Select an image with social or cultural meaning. Describe the rhetorical situation and explain the rhetorical strategies used to convey its message.

REFERENCES

Aristotle. (1994-1998). *Rhetoric*. (W. Rhys Roberts, Trans.) https://www.bocc.ubi.pt/pag/Aristotle-rhetoric.pdf

Bazerman, C. (2013). *A Rhetoric of Literate Action: Literate Action Volume 1*. WAC Clearinghouse. https://doi.org/10.37514/PER-B.2013.0513

Bitzer, L.F. (1968). The Rhetorical Situation. *Philosophy and Rhetoric. 1* (1), pp. 1-14. https://www.jstor.org/stable/40236733

Bratta, P. and Powell, M. (2016, April 20). Introduction to the Special Issue: Entering the Cultural Rhetorics Conversations. *Enculturation: A Journal of Rhetoric, Writing, and Culture*. https://enculturation.net/entering-the-cultural-rhetorics-conversations

Cronkhite, T. (n.d.) 7. Kairos. *Rhetorical Choices*. Aims Community College.https://pressbooks.pub/words/chapter/chapter-7-kairos/

Duffy, W. (2023). What is Rhetoric? A "Choose Your Own Adventure" Primer. (T. Daniels-Lerberg,D. Driscoll, M.K. Stewart, M. Vetter, Ed.) *Writing Spaces: Readings on Writing, Volume 5* (pp. 247-265) WAC Clearinghouse. https://wac.colostate.edu/docs/books/writingspaces5/15Duffy.pdf

Gagich, M. and Zickel, E. (n.d.). 6.4 Rhetorical Appeals: Logos, Pathos, and Ethos Defined. *A Guide to Rhetoric, Genre, and Success in First-Year Writing*. MSL Academic Endeavors.https://pressbooks.ulib.csuohio.edu/csu-fyw-rhetoric/chapter/rhetorical-strategies-build ng-compelling-arguments/

Hall, S. (1997). Introduction, In S. Hall (Ed.), *Representation: Cultural Representations and Signifying Practices* (pp. 1-11). SAGE Publications.

King, M. L, Jr. (2010). *I Have a Dream* [speech transcript]. NPR.https://www.npr.org/2010/01/18/122701268/i-have-a-dream-speech-in-its-entirety.

McNulty, B. (2021). The Ability of Identity: An Ever-Changing Word, In A. Von Berg (Ed.), *Rhetoric in Everyday Life.* Library Partners Press. https://librarypartnerspress.pressbooks.pub/rhetoricineverydaylife/chapter/the-ability-of-identity-an-ever-changing-word-by-braxton-mcnulty/#:~:text=While%20somebody%27s%20personal%20definition%20of,relationships%20are%20formed%20in%20society

"Popular and Commercial Culture." (2018, June 7) National Park Service.https://www.nps.gov/stli/learn/historyculture/statue-adn-popular-culture.htm

Sackett & Wilhelms Corp, N.Y. (1917). *American WWI Poster: Remember Your First Thrill of AMERICAN LIBERTY OUR DUTY - But United States Government Bonds 2nd Liberty Loan of 1917* [Advertisement]. Retrieved May 5, 2024, from https://commons.wikipedia.org/wiki/File:Novum_Eboracum.jpg.

Sutch, R. (2015, December 4). *Liberty Bonds.* Federal Reserve History. https://www.federalreservehistory.org/essays/liberty-bonds

CHAPTER 5
GUIDED BY GENRE
Genevieve Mills

CHAPTER OUTCOMES
- Develop an understanding of genre and how to recognize different genres of writing.
- Recognize how to adapt your writing to suit different genres.
- Acquire techniques to adjust your reading to suit different genres.

KEY TERMS
- Genre
- Genre Conventions
- Reading Rhetorically

CHAPTER OVERVIEW

This chapter gives students an understanding of genre and how to recognize different genres of writing. It covers how to adapt your writing and reading to suit different genres. It describes why it's important to be able to recognize what genre you're reading and writing in order to be a better reader and writer.

GENRE AWARENESS

Lightning cracks across the night sky, illuminating a crumbling mansion. Shutters with peeling paint slam in the wind and startle the two young women tiptoeing down a cobwebbed hallway. When they realize the noise was just the shutters, they laugh it off and keep going toward the closed door at the end of the hallway. A low growl comes from the door, but a thunderclap masks it, and the women keep walking. One of them places a hand on the doorknob. She shivers and looks back at the other woman, who nods at her.

You yell at the screen at the women not to open the door that there's definitely danger lurking behind the rotted wood, but of course, they don't listen. They open the door and are immediately attacked by a spectral figure. You shake your head at their stupidity as the movie continues, following other, smarter characters.

How did you know that the women would find trouble behind the door? Is it because you're psychic? No, you knew you were watching a horror movie, and you knew in horror movies, on dark and stormy nights in old houses, ghosts hide behind closed doors. You could predict what would happen because you're familiar with the horror genre.

We engage with many different genres every day. Your Spotify Wrapped listed your favorite genres of music; when you're choosing what to watch on Netflix, you may sort by genre, and instead of aimlessly wandering the aisles of a bookstore, you go straight for the sign with your favorite genre written on it. But genre doesn't just apply to media.

Genre is also a way to look at writing. In composition, genre helps us set expectations so that we're more prepared when we're given a writing assignment or so we can better understand what we read. This chapter will first define genre and reading rhetorically in order to better understand the terms we're using before explaining why being aware of genre is important, and how to better understand genre expectations. After we become familiar with genre, we'll look at some examples of different genres of writing to demonstrate the concept.

DEFINING GENRE

Simply put, a *genre* of writing is a form of writing. Each piece of writing within that form follows specific patterns or conventions to fulfill its goals. Genres are ways of recognizing and responding to other writing (Bawarshi & Reiff, 2010). Unless you're writing something no one else will ever read, your writing will have an audience. And that audience will have expectations based on what else they've read, so when defining genre, we also look at how those expectations have developed. Carolyn Miller (1984) argued, "...a rhetorically sound definition of genre must be centered not on the substance or the form of discourse but on the action it is used to accomplish" (p. 151). In defining a genre, we must look at the *why* instead of just the what. Genres aren't just categories of writing but also situations and motives (Miller, 1984).

While you may think you only know one form of writing, you absolutely already know many different forms and can switch between them with ease. Think about texting. A text is one writing genre. When you're composing a text, you follow different conventions than you do when you're writing a resumé. When you're texting, you probably don't end the last sentence with a period. Maybe you don't use any punctuation. You probably have a lot of incomplete sentences. You may use emojis or gifs and have a lot of abbreviations and slang. Whereas if you're writing a resumé, you end each sentence with a period. You start with your name and address, followed by a heading for your education, followed by another heading for your job history and skills. You're certainly not adding gifs or emojis, and you're probably not using any slang.

So why do you write in different ways when you write a text versus a resumé? It's because you're familiar with both genres: texts and resumés. You know the *genre conventions* or the common characteristics used in each form. You know that if you started texting a friend with perfect punctuation, they're going to start wondering if you've been kidnapped and someone else is using your phone, and you know you don't need to add a heading with your name and address at the top of each text because your friend already has your name saved in their phone. Similarly, you know that emojis aren't going to go over well with the HR person reading your resumé. You're considering your situation and motive for writing in both examples.

While trying to determine what the conventions of a genre are, you can ask these questions from Braziller & Kleinfeld (2020):
- How does the author guide the readers through the piece? What methods do they use to get their points across?
- How do word choice, the use of literary devices like metaphors, and other stylistic techniques work to engage readers?
- How do design elements, such as color, images, and font, emphasize the author's purpose?

- What types of sources are cited and how? If there aren't sources, why do you think that is?
- If you can answer these questions, both your reading and writing will improve.

We write in different ways depending on what we're trying to accomplish with that piece of writing, be it communicating a joke or getting a job, as well as changing how we write based on who we are writing to, so a friend or a hiring manager, and in what context, digital or on paper. That is to say, when we write, we consider our purpose, audience, and context. Right now, you may feel unfamiliar with different genres of academic writing, which may lead to insecurities when writing. But with more experience reading different types of academic writing, you'll gain genre awareness and, therefore, confidence when writing. According to Jacobson (2021):

> When we repeatedly encounter texts within a genre, we get a sense of the language and content they tend to use, as well as how they arrange that language and content. Successful writers have a good idea of how to write effectively in particular genres—this means satisfying readers' expectations for the genre but maybe also making a text fresh and interesting. (pp. 218-219)

Understanding genre is important to understanding writing itself because when you're aware of genre, you're aware of audience, purpose, and expectations. You'll be able to understand why writers write the way they write and examine how effective your own writing is. To examine effectiveness, you'll have to learn to read rhetorically, as we'll discuss in the next section.

GENRE AWARENESS AND RHETORIC READING

If you've started thinking about genre, you've already started thinking rhetorically because you're thinking about how a piece of writing works. When you read rhetorically, you apply what you know about genre to a piece of writing (also called a text). Instead of just thinking about plot or content, "one who reads rhetorically seeks to understand how meaning in a text is shaped not only by the text itself, but also the context" (Gagich & Zickel, 2018). *Reading rhetorically* means looking not just at what the author writes but also at how they've organized their writing and why (Gagich & Zickel, 2018). Thinking of the context involves looking at what genres the writing may fit into, while considering the author's identity, who the intended audience is and their interests and needs, the medium the author is writing in, the reason for creating the text, and more.

WHEN TRYING TO READ RHETORICALLY, YOU CAN ASK THESE QUESTIONS:

- Who is the author?
  You can try and find out about the author's background by looking up what else they've written, if they're an expert in the topic they're writing on, and what their

job is. A journalist is going to have a different approach to writing than a professor or a novelist.
- When and where was the text published?
Knowing where something was published helps you identify its purpose. It may also let you know if there may be some biases in the writing. Knowing when something was published is important because cultural norms change over time.
- What is the author's main purpose?
The author's purpose is what they want to accomplish with the text. It's the reason they're writing at all. The goal could be to persuade readers to gain a new point of view or act differently. The goal could be to inform or entertain.
- Who is the audience?
Who is the author writing to, and what does the author think of their audience? Knowing your audience is important because you'll choose different words depending on who you're writing to. Think back to the texting example. You may use "lol" when texting friends but maybe not when texting your grandparents because they won't know what it means.
- How is the text organized, and why is it organized that way?
What style does the writing follow? This could mean citation style, looking at APA versus MLA, or you could look at what information the text starts with. Is it the most important information or the most exciting? Can you find a thesis statement, and if so, where is it?

Asking yourself these questions while reading means you're reading rhetorically and considering genre as you read. You'll be a more informed and careful reader, and with practice, will have an easier time understanding different texts as you learn why people write the way they write.

WHY GENRE MATTERS

Genre awareness doesn't just mean you know how to write in a particular genre. You also understand how a given genre achieves its purposes and how the different parts of a text, the writer, the intended reader, and the text itself, are informed by purpose. This is more than just memorizing form and imitating it. It's understanding the why and how of different genres.

Going back to the horror movie example, why are so many horror movies set during thunderstorms? Is it because there's something inherently scary about thunder and lightning? Or is it because the sounds of a storm can cover up other noises and can trap characters in a building without power?

If you're familiar with a genre, you can think critically about the choices made in each genre. According to Clark (2011):

> Without genre awareness, [students] will not understand how the text "works" to fulfill its purpose, and when they encounter a new genre in another course, they may lack the tools to engage with it effectively, which explains why students fall back so fixedly on the omnipresent five-paragraph essay. (p. 67)

The five-paragraph essay is fine. You probably learned it in high school, and it worked as a form of writing for a while. But becoming familiar with other essay genres is a way to break away from the five-paragraph essay that may have been limiting your writing. You can move beyond that form once you understand why that form works. And why does it work? The five-paragraph essay consists of an introduction, three body paragraphs, and a conclusion. The introduction is crucial because it gives readers important background information, grabs their attention, and introduces the thesis or purpose of the essay. Each body paragraph is focused around one argument that directly supports the thesis. Teachers emphasize three supporting arguments because that creates a relatively simple but compelling thesis. "I think THIS because of THIS, THIS, and, THIS." And a conclusion works because it forces you to reconsider your supporting arguments and thesis as you restate them, so that you have time to make sure you're making your point as clear as possible. Once you're as familiar with the genre of the five-paragraph essay as you are with the genre of texting a friend, you'll ideally feel as comfortable writing an essay as you do a text.

But this strict form isn't the only way to write an essay with a thesis. Your thesis may be more complex and require more than three supporting arguments. Or your supporting arguments may be more complex and require whole paragraphs detailing specific examples. If you're aware of your purpose in writing the essay and of the genre of the essay you're trying to write, you can pick which conventions best serve your purpose and which you can ignore. Don't let a genre box you in. Much as grammar rules should serve the speaker, not the other way around, so too should grammar conventions serve the writer. Think of them as tools in your toolbox. While you may not need both a hammer and screwdriver to assemble a piece of furniture, it's nice to have both handy. According to Devitt (2009): "Genres are social and rhetorical actions: they develop their languages and forms out of rhetorical aims and contexts shared by groups" (p. 346). We contribute to genres as we write in them, and we can pick and choose which genre conventions we follow.

When you're given an essay prompt, examine it carefully. Ideally, the prompt will tell you what type of essay the professor wants or what genre of essay they want. If you're familiar with that genre, writing the essay will be much easier. If you're unfamiliar with it, it's time to study. Look for examples of the genre. If you're writing a personal narrative, read other personal narratives and examine what moves the writers make. Right away, you'll notice that in each personal narrative, the writer uses first-person, or "I" and "me," so now you know that you can also use first-person to write your personal narrative. You may read five personal narratives and notice that four of them start in the middle of a scene with dialogue. This is an effective move because it catches readers' attention and engages them right away. You may decide to use this same move in your own personal narrative, and now you're engaging with genre conventions.

In addition to using genre awareness to classify the different types of writing you might do, genre matters because you can use your awareness to classify various kinds of sources you will come across as you research and read. Writing and reading skills build on each other. Understanding one helps improve your knowledge of the other. Improving your skill at reading different genres will likely enhance your skill at writing different genres and vice-versa.

Understanding genres will also help you to become a better researcher. Throughout your college courses, you will have to study various periodical publications, and understanding how each works will help you find the information you're looking for faster. This is because "systems of genres provide a concept for understanding the way interrelated genres constitute specific networks of social action" (Carter, 2007, p. 392). Understanding a genre means understanding how writers work in conversation with each other and how you can add to that conversation with your writing.

RECOGNIZING GENRES

You're never going to master all genres, but still, learning about genres and how they function is important. When you encounter a new genre, first look for multiple examples of it. If it's a relatively public genre, you can find samples easily through an internet search. For more specialized genres, you may need to look in textbooks and manuals about the genre or specialized databases. Try and find as many samples as possible because, as Bawarshi and Reiff (2010) put it, "The more samples of the genre you collect, the more you will be able to notice patterns within the genre" (p. 193). The patterns that emerge will help you determine the genre conventions.

If you have to write in a new genre, determine what you're trying to accomplish and who your audience is. Look back at the rhetorical reading questions and determine what rhetorical moves you should make in your writing. If your professor gives you specific guidelines, of course, you should follow them, but beyond that, try and decide how you should write based on what you're trying to achieve (beyond a good grade). Are you trying to convince your reader to agree with your point of view? Or are you trying to educate them? What's the best way to get your point across?

EXAMPLES OF GENRE

In this class, we write in 4 genres: narrative, genre analysis, opinion editorials, and reflections. We'll briefly look at the audience and conventions for each.

NARRATIVE ESSAY

The conventions of a narrative essay are in the name. A narrative essay follows a narrative, which is to say, it has a narrative arc, or a beginning, middle, and end. It's a short story, but usually a true story. Narrative essays are very similar to short stories. They have characters, scenes with dialogue, settings, and themes. If it's a personal narrative, you're writing about yourself, so you're the main character and can use first-person throughout. Even if it's not an essay about yourself, you may be a side character in the story and it's from your point of view. Narrative essays should still have a clear purpose, even if they don't have an explicit thesis statement.

Introductions for narrative essays vary. They often start with an exciting moment in scene, but can also start with exposition to set the stage for what's to come. They typically have some sort of hook to grab readers' attention. Even if your audience is your professor who has to read your essay, it's still best practice to try to make it engaging.

GENRE ANALYSIS

A genre analysis uses rhetorical reading to examine a text. You're writing about the author's goals, techniques, and appeals to the audience. Genre analysis conventions typically include an introduction presenting the thesis, body paragraphs that analyze the text directly, and a conclusion to summarize your main ideas and wrap up any arguments you may have made.

A rhetorical analysis attempts to be more objective than a narrative. It typically doesn't use first-person language. It often quotes from the text and, therefore, has a list of references that follows a citation style guide. The language in a theoretical analysis is usually formal and academic because your audience is other writers engaged in genre analysis, who know the basics and are reading your work to enhance their own understanding.

OPINION EDITORIALS

Opinion editorials balance both opinion and fact. Their purpose is to influence public opinion, encourage critical thinking, and sometimes make people take action on a social issue. An editorial uses well-sourced facts to back up the author's opinion on a subject. Editorials usually have an introduction with a hook, a body with evidence, and a conclusion that summarizes the author's views, like other essays. They may also explain the issue being addressed as objectively as possible, then present counter-arguments and the writer's opinions. They're less formal than a rhetorical analysis and may use first-person language to express the writer's views more directly.

The audience for opinion editorials varies, so it's important to determine who your audience is when writing one. An editorial for a local paper on why a new bike lane should be added to Main Street has a very different audience than a New York Times editorial on the president. You should determine how much prior knowledge your audience has. Do you need to define some terms you may consider basic but your audience doesn't? Or would defining the basics annoy your readers by wasting their time? If you know your audience you'll know the best way to reach them through your writing.

REFLECTIONS

Reflections are a genre of writing that asks you to think about your own thinking or write about your own writing (Giles, 2010). Your instructor may give you specific questions to answer or just ask you to reflect on the writing process in general, in which case you may have to ask yourself some questions, like what was your intention with the essay or what decisions were you made regarding word choice and sentence structure?

Your audience is, of course, yourself and your professor, but perhaps also your classmates you're writing the reflection before a peer review. In which case, you need to make any issues you're having with your writing clear. You can use specific terms you've discussed in class since your peers and professor are familiar with them. Your purpose is to help your instructor or peers give you better feedback (Giles, 2010).

DISCUSSION QUESTIONS AND ACTIVITIES

1. What's your favorite genre of music? How do you recognize that genre? What are a few things all the songs in that genre have in common?
2. What is a writing genre you use regularly in your daily life? What are the conventions?
3. What is a writing genre you have used as a student? What are the conventions?
4. How would you define the term "genre?"
5. How does genre awareness, its conventions, and expectations help you as a writer?

REFERENCES

Bawarshi, A., & Reiff, M. J. (2010). *Genre: An introduction to history, theory, research, and pedagogy.* https://openlibrary.org/books/OL24099291M/Genre

Braziller, A., & Kleinfeld, E. (2020). *The Bedford book of genres: A guide and reader.* Bedford Books.

Carter, M. (2007). Ways of knowing, doing, and writing in the disciplines. *College Composition and Communication, 58*(3), 385–418. http://www.jstor.org/stable/20456952

Clark, I. L., & Hernandez, A. (2011). Genre awareness, academic argument, and transferability. *The WAC Journal, 22*(1), 65–78. https://doi.org/10.37514/wac-j.2011.22.1.05

Devitt, A. J. (2009). *Teaching critical genre awareness.* In *The WAC Clearinghouse; Parlor Press eBooks,* 341–354. https://doi.org/10.37514/per-b.2009.2324.2.17

Gagich, M., & Zickel, E. (2018). *A guide to rhetoric, genre, and success in first-year writing.* MSL Academic Endeavors Imprint of Michael Schwartz Library at Cleveland State University. https://pressbooks.ulib.csuohio.edu/csu-fyw-rhetoric/

Giles, S. L. (2010). Reflective writing and the revision process: What were you thinking? In C. Lowe & P. Zemliansky (Eds.), *Writing Spaces: Readings on Writing* (pp. 191–204). Parlor Press. https://writingspaces.org/past-volumes/reflective-writing-and-the-revision-process-what-were-you-thinking/

Jacobson, B., Pawlowski, M., & Tardy, C. (2021). Make your "move": Writing in genres. In C. Lowe & P. Zemliansky (Eds.), *Writing Spaces: Readings on Writing* (217-238). Parlor Press.

Miller, C. L. (1984). Genre as social action. *Quarterly journal of speech, 70*(2), 151–167. https://doi.org/10.1080/00335638409383686

CHAPTER 6
GIVING CREDIT WHERE CREDIT IS DUE
Erika J. Pichardo

CHAPTER OUTCOMES
- The Ethics Behind Citing and Avoiding Plagiarism Understand Information Literacy
- Understand Information Literacy
- How to Become Comfortable Working with Sources
- The Role AI Plays in our Academic Writing

KEY TERMS
- Academic Integrity
- Information literacy
- Citing
- Plagiarism
- Ethics
- Artificial intelligence

CHAPTER OVERVIEW

This chapter explores writing with sources. It is a review of academic integrity and how that plays into thinking in writing. Then, there is a discussion on information literacy and how to develop those skills as writers. As part of the college experience, there will be interactions with other writers with both similar and different interests. This is to be expected as contextual and verbal skills develop and comfort increases in joining and writing conversations in this class and beyond. Learning how to engage with various texts allows consideration for the legitimacy and credibility of these sources, and how to integrate a writer's voice, either through primary or secondary sources, to strengthen one's arguments and confirm others. First is the definition of plagiarism and discussion on how Pace University defines it. Then, there is a discussion of the ethics behind citing, which defines, the importance of ethics and academic integrity in the world of writing; avoiding plagiarism which outlines the various ways to cite to become more comfortable with using reputable and multiple sources; understanding the importance of information literacy, and how to become comfortable working with sources; and the role AI plays in academic writing.

ETHICS OF CITATION AND AVOIDING PLAGIARISM

College writing requires students to express their opinions and integrate these thoughts into ongoing academic discussions across a wide range of fields of study. Through summaries, quotes, and paraphrases, student writers include source material to confirm their points of view and/or present new ways of thinking. Adding sources and evidence allows writers to deepen their own understanding and increase credibility with their readers or audience. When students engage with the contributions other writers and authors make to a topic, they must adhere to standards of academic integrity, "the commitment to and demonstration of honest and moral behavior in an academic setting" (The Writing Center, University of North Carolina at Chapel Hill, 2024, para. 1). At the root of this practice is "the ethical use of information, thoughts, and ideas from which we build original thought to contribute to the academic conversation" (The University of Arizona, 2023, para. 3). Being ethical students and writers relates directly to academic integrity, the practice of taking responsibility for submitted work, acknowledging the work of others, and giving credit where credit is due (Teaching & Learning, Ohio State University Libraries, 2015).

Plagiarism is neglecting to recognize the contributions of others. At Pace University[1], students are expected to practice academic integrity, honesty, and ethics as they satisfy their academic requirements (Pace University, 2017). While plagiarism is a serious offense that may carry severe consequences, the purpose of this chapter is not to create anxious writers. It is not a cautionary tale of what happens when a student cheats, either. Pace, Pleasantville writing instructors do not believe their students are by nature deceptive. They are not there to police students or their work. Rather, writing professors are aware that students plagiarize unintentionally when they do not know how to properly cite sources and intentionally when they feel overwhelmed by a class or classes and are unsure how to be successful. This chapter is a teaching opportunity, one moment of many when writing faculty will provide instruction to help students become more comfortable with properly integrating sources into their academic writing.

THE IMPORTANCE OF INFORMATION LITERACY

Part of writing is learning how to move from an opinion-based approach to an evidence-based approach when writing about a topic. This allows the reader to recognize the writer has done their due diligence to ensure their opinion of a topic is supported by evidence provided by other writers. Becoming a writer is a process, and part of that process is developing one's ability to gather and interpret information. The American Library Association (2024) defines information literacy as recognizing when information is needed, being able to evaluate that information, and to understand when to use it effectively in one's argument. It is the ability to use multiple senses and skills to determine what to use to support and strengthen writing skills.

Whenever given writing assignments, students begin to think about what they know related to that assignment. Students look over the prompt and highlight what the instructor is looking for. This ranges from formatting, to genre, to number of sources. This is the beginning of practicing information literacy. Students look at the prompt for the assignment and read it to ensure they understand exactly what is expected of them to write about, what evidence they want to add as support for their arguments, and how to format

---

[1] Pace University's Academic Integrity Code (2017) specifically defines plagiarism as "the adoption or reproduction of ideas or words or statements of another person as one's own without acknowledgment. This would include, for example, copying the answers of another person or copying or substantially restating the published, unpublished, or on-line work of another person without appropriate attribution, or collaborating with another person on an academic endeavor without the prior knowledge of the instructor or without proper acknowledgment of the other person's contribution" (p. 1).

Chapter 6: Giving Credit Where Credit is Due

the assignment, all before the submission date. These steps allow the opportunity to seek, an understanding of the assignment, evaluate what the stance will be on the topic, and use sources of information to help create and support the writer's goal and stance.

Information literacy is how students begin to feel comfortable with sources because they begin to use their analytical and technical skills to determine the value of a source in respect to their stance in the writing space. Information literacy gives the skills to find reputable sources so students can scan, read, and interpret texts effectively (Burnell et al., 2020). Reputable sources are those which have been evaluated and written by experts in the field. This becomes even more important as sources become available online and develop into the digital age. Understanding information literacy is the first step. Now that the basis has been set up on understanding how these terms relate to using analytical and technical skills, it is time to investigate how to become comfortable with using these sources.

BECOMING COMFORTABLE WITH SOURCES AND CITING

Becoming comfortable with sources and citing means becoming comfortable with what to look for to determine whether a source is reputable. Becoming comfortable with a source and determining it is reputable is the first step, delving into how to react to those sources and how to cite. Sources generally fall under two categories: peer-reviewed or not peer-reviewed. Peer-review, also known as scholarly sources, undergo a lengthy publication process, include extensive lists of references, and write with their intended audience in mind, usually those in their field (Purdue Owl, 2024). Much of these sources can be found in books and journals. The opposite of a scholarly source would be a popular source, where the publication process is not as extensive and publication does not require a list of references along with submission (Purdue Owl, 2024). Sources that fall under scholarly and peer-review, then, are more reliable sources of evidence.

When determining whether a source is reliable, there are a few things you can investigate. First, who is the author(s)? Are they experts in the field? Have they published before or do they work in the field? This is important because this also helps to remove sources from your view written by those who are not experts in the field. Next, look where the source is published. Is it published on a website? Is it published in a chapter of a book? Is it published in a journal? If found in a journal, did you access that journal through a database and was that source peer-reviewed? Once you determine where it is published, investigate if those journals, webpages, or books are reputable and can be used to support your evidence.

Now, you can begin to look at the text itself. Are they using sources to support their own argument? Is the support they use unbiased, meaning are the sources being used as evidence for the argument being discussed? Sources should be used to accurately support the argument of the research rather than supporting the researcher. Are they citing correctly and including a reference page? These questions allow you to focus on the source's external material so you feel more comfortable once you start to read the source for its information.

You have your sources, now what? Students may feel overwhelmed reading sources with so much information that you begin to question, "Well, what is my focus on?" To determine what your focus should be on, think about what you are trying to answer. Allow your questions to guide you in choosing sources related to your topic area. This will help you create a list of sources focused on your topic area to start reading and honing into choosing sources which will help answer that question and connect your opinions to evidence. When looking for sources, you should look in scholarly databases, reputable websites, and educational agencies. Once you find your sources, The first step is annotation or journaling what you are reading. Doing this allows you to react to what you're reading, focus on what you've learned, and reflect how it relates to the assignment (Bazerman, 2010). This gives you autonomy as a reader and allows you to focus on what you feel is important to reflect in your own assignment. Additionally, when you annotate all your sources and journal all your reactions, you notice similarities among the sources related to arguments or even references used. Once you annotate and journal your sources, you can begin to think how you want to cite. There are three ways to incorporate sources—direct quoting, paraphrasing, summarizing—and they are reviewed below.

Direct quotation means taking the exact words and phrases written by the author and adding them to the assignment. If choosing to directly quote, it is essential to include the author(s), page or paragraph number, and quotation marks. The quotation marks indicate to the reader the information being presented is coming from a specific article or book to add support to the assignment, and the author(s) and page or paragraph numbers indicate, where exactly the reader can read this information from. Including this information ensures proper citation to avoid plagiarizing. It is appropriate to use direct quotations when the author's word choice and context will help the reader fully understand the importance of this author's argument. Choosing to add a direct quote ensures the author's emphasis and meaning are not minimized. A perfect example of this is when I offered the definition of plagiarism for Pace University. I directly quoted because I wanted to ensure you know this is the exact definition Pace uses when determining what is or is not plagiarism.

Paraphrasing is when you want to put the author's thoughts into one's own words. When you paraphrase, you use one's words to express the same meaning as the author. When paraphrasing, consider Bazerman's (2010) steps:

1. Read the original text thoroughly;
2. As you substitute the words and phrases, ask yourself if the meaning as the author has not changed by changing the words or structure;
3. Once you paraphrase, check what you wrote against what you read again to ensure the meaning has not changed; and
4. Cite correctly by including the necessary information. Because this is not a direct quotation, a page or paragraph number is not needed since these are your own words representing the meaning of the author.

After writing your paraphrase, be sure to compare what you havewritten to the original text. Your obligation is not to simply cite the author. You must also maintain the integrity of what the author was saying - their intent. Therefore, you cannot stray from the author's meaning or main point. By reviewing and comparing the original text in your paraphrase, you are ensuring the information being paraphrased is an accurate representation of the original author's message (Bazerman, 2010).

The next form of citation, summarizing, is great to use to show similarities across multiple sources or compress a large body of text into a few sentences. When directly quoting, the language and message of the author are important. When paraphrasing, the message of the author are important. When summarizing, the message is important because what is being supported is referenced in multiple sources (Bazerman, 2010). Because the focus of a summary is on what was written rather than how it was written, this is really where the author expresses similarities across multiple sources. When several sources express similar stances, this is known as synthesizing (Bazerman, 2010). Being able to synthesize showcases not only one's comfort with sources and citing but also with information literacy. It showcases the skills of annotating, journaling, and making inferences about similarities in multiple sources. Citing summaries is very similar to paraphrasing as it includes the author(s) names, but since summarizing involves multiple sources, all authors from all sources must be cited. Multiple citations indicate this information can be found in multiple sources supporting the main argument of the paper being written. Bazerman (2010) and Purdue Owl (2024) both discuss the importance of evaluation and objectivity when looking at articles; these two sources both emphasize the importance of evaluation when reading articles and determining reliability. This is an example where summarizing the information found in both sources indicates the importance of evaluation when determining reliability of sources and creating a summary of sources.

Sources and citing can be fun once students feel comfortable in the process. Looking for sources and ensuring quality is a continuous process, especially as technology and access evolve. Next is a discussion around the role of artificial intelligence (AI) in the last section of this chapter, which really emphasizes these changes.

AI AND ACADEMIC WRITING

Although the conversation around AI has recently become ubiquitous, it was born in the 1950s with the introduction of the Turing test to determine if machines could think (IBM, 2024). Since then, AI has grown and evolved, leaving some supportive, fearful, or aware of its benefits and drawbacks. This section does not provide a position[2]. Rather, I consider the relationship between Gen AI, academic integrity, use of sources, and development of writing.

AI cannot be used as a replacement for one's own writing and evaluation process since it does not allow for an academic process which involves the author. The author determines the argumentative stance, evaluates the sources, determines reliability, and introduces those reliable sources into their writing. Gen AI would be considered a plagiarism tool when used to develop your work. Such software, however, may be critically and ethically integrated into academic writing, such as brainstorming (Northwestern University, 2023; Wang, 2022) or organizational tool (Kansas University, n.d.). AI expectations often operate on a class-by-class basis, so be sure to engage with faculty about their position on its use. Still, students should be aware of the following:
- AI cannot replace the thought process of a human. That means, AI will not be able to understand what you truly want to communicate as it does not have a personality or a voice like a human writing would have (Manivannan, 2023).
- Where humans can be creative, AI lacks that process to add necessary detail and be organized and purposeful in genre selection (Manivannan, 2023).

---
2 Program AI Policy included in course syllabus.

- AI use may result in "reduced critical thinking and problem-solving skills" and "decreased engagement and motivation in learning" (Dempsey, 2023, para. 1).
- AI cannot guarantee its sources are accurate or unbiased, which calls into question if material is reputable (University of Illinois, 2024).

As the technical world continues to evolve, the hope is to use it as a supportive measure but not lose the creative or academic notion of what it means to write. It is important not to lose creative processes and ability to make connections as human intellect allows; this is where students can stay organized in their thoughts, express their opinions, and use evidence to support an argumentative stance. Thoughts and opinions are important, and the only way to continue individual expressions is by continuing to write using one's own words, phrases, and comprehension.

CONCLUSION

This chapter focused on the ethics behind citing and avoiding plagiarism, understanding the importance of information literacy, how to become comfortable working with sources, and the role AI plays in academic writing. The goal of this chapter was to help reduce the fear of plagiarism by defining what can be done to ensure proper citation. Further, there is a connection to ethics behind citing to ensure academic integrity. Lastly, I concluded with a review of AI and its relationship to academic writing, noting this is an ongoing conversation as technology continues to develop and evolve.

DISCUSSION QUESTIONS

1. In your own words, what is academic integrity?
2. Go to the institution's library database and look for an article. How can you tell if this source is reputable?
3. Read *Pace University Academic Integrity Code*. After reading, practice creating a direct quote, a paraphrase, and a summary.
4. What are your thoughts on AI and writing? How might AI affect your writing?
5. What are some ethical considerations of AI? As a writer? As a reader?

REFERENCES

American Library Association. (2024). Information literacy. https://literacy.ala.org/information-literacy/

Bazerman, C. (2010). *The informed writer: Using sources in the disciplines*. The WAC Clearinghouse. https://wac.colostate.edu/books/practice/informedwriter/

Burnell, C., Wood, J., Babin, M., Pesznecker, S., & Rosevear, N. (2020). *The word on college reading and writing*. Center for Open Education University of Minnesota. https://openoregon.pressbooks.pub/wrd/

Dempsey, J. (2023, January 18). *AI: Arguing its Place in Higher Education*. Higher Education Digest. https://www.highereducationdigest.com/ai-arguing-its-place-in-higher-education/

IBM. (2024). *What is artificial intelligence (AI)*. https://www.ibm.com/topics/artificial-intelligence

Kansas University. (n.d.). *Using AI Ethically in Writing Assignments*. https://cte.ku.edu/ethical-use-ai-writing-assignments

Manivannan, V. (n.d.). *Statement on AI and Writing*. Pace University Writing-Enhanced Course Program Guidebook. chrome-extension://efaidnbmnnnibpcajpcglclefindmkaj/https://www.pace.edu/sites/default/files/2023-09/dyson-writing-enhanced-courses-guidebook.pdf

Northwestern University. (2023, November 30). *Using AI tools in your research.* https://libguides.northwestern.edu/ai-tools-research/acad-integ

Pace University. (2017, September 1). *Pace University academic integrity code.* https://www.pace.edu/sites/default/files/files/student-handbook/pace-university-academic-integrity-code.pdf

Purdue Owl. (2024). *Evaluating sources: Where to begin.* Purdue University. https://owl.purdue.edu/owl/research_and_citation/conducting_research/evaluating_sources_of_information/where_to_begin.html

Teaching & Learning, University Libraries. (2015). *Choosing & using sources: A guide to academic research.* The Ohio State University. https://ohiostate.pressbooks.pub/choosingsources/

The University of Arizona. (2023). *What is academic integrity, and how can I achieve it?* University of Arizona Global Campus. https://www.uagc.edu/blog/what-is-academic-integrity-and-how-can-i-achieve-it#:~:text=your%20college%20assignments.-,What%20is%20Academic%20Integrity%3F,contribute%20to%20the%20academic%20conversation.%E2%80%9D

The Writing Center. (2024). *Academic integrity.* University of North Carolina at Chapel Hill. https://writingcenter.unc.edu/esl/resources/academic-integrity/

University of Illinois-Champaign. (2024, October 24). *AI in Schools: Pros and Cons.* https://education.illinois.edu/about/news-events/news/article/2024/10/24/ai-in-schools--pros-and-cons

Wang, Z. (2022). Computer-assisted EFL writing and evaluations based on artificial intelligence: a case from a college reading and writing course. *Library Hi Tech, 40*(1), 80–97. https://doi.org/10.1108/LHT-05-2020-0113

CHAPTER 7

ENGAGING WRITERS IN A DIALOGUE OF REVISION

Zac Ginsburg

CHAPTER OUTCOMES

- Understand the value of constructive criticism and praise comments.
- Describe specific techniques for giving writing feedback to peers.
- Reflect on how to address feedback in your own writing.
- Understand the value of a growth mindset in the feedback process.

KEY TERMS

- Praise
- Constructive criticism
- Higher-order concerns
- Lower-order concerns
- Growth mindset
- Fixed mindset

CHAPTER OVERVIEW

This chapter discusses how to give feedback to peers on their writing. It breaks down different types of feedback and shows how to use these techniques, with examples from a real student's writing. By the end of the chapter, you should feel prepared to participate in a workshop or peer review. There are also some tips for what to do with the feedback you receive.

OF TWO MINDS

The thought of giving a classmate feedback on their writing can be intimidating. What if I offend someone? What if I have nothing to say? Will the writer even take my suggestions seriously? These concerns are completely understandable, especially if you have little or no experience in writing workshops. As someone who has participated in countless workshops as a student and facilitated them as a teacher, I am confident that you will develop the skills to give quality feedback and use the feedback you receive in the best way possible to improve your writing.

Richard Straub (1999), a professor who dedicated his career to examining feedback practices, said, "Be always of two (or three) minds about your response to the paper" (p. 140). The two minds Straub refers to are praise and criticism. With these two minds, you can approach any type of workshop or peer review with confidence. In this essay, you'll learn how to offer meaningful praise, give thoughtful, constructive criticism, and use the feedback you receive to make changes to your papers.

THE IMPORTANCE OF PRAISE

My hands were shaking. I was reading my short story aloud to my entire class. This was an introduction to fiction course at Wesleyan University, but none of my classmates seemed like beginners. During their workshops, when they read their own writing aloud, it was as if beautiful language had poured from their brains straight onto the page. Not me. I was reading my choppy story about teenage boys getting mugged in a park in Chicago, where I grew up. It was a dumb idea. My first ever short story. Help!

As I read, I tried to make my voice louder than the sound of my classmates' pens, scribbling notes on their printed copies of my story. My mouth was dry. I more or less blacked out, having no idea what part of the story I was reading from, just reciting one word after another until it was done. Please let it be done.

I feared the worst, but what I learned, as I came back to consciousness, was that my classmates did not eviscerate me. That's because the teacher started the discussion of my story with praise. At first, I thought my classmates were lying, but after two, three, then five praise comments, I began to crawl out of my cave of self-doubt. By telling me that they liked the mood I created with my descriptions of the eerie lamplit park at night or that they could feel the angst of my teenage protagonist, they showed me that they were engaging with my writing and that parts of it worked for them. It felt good. Eventually, the praise ended, and we turned toward constructive criticism, but by that point, it felt more like a conversation than a heap of judgment. I was open to hearing how they thought I could improve.

Peter Elbow (1998), a professor who's written extensively on the topic of feedback, refers to this as the "believing game" (p. 148). Instead of reading my story with the goal of poking holes in it and pointing out flaws, my classmates attempted to see my vision for the story. By trying their best to believe in what I was writing, they could guide me toward what I hoped the story would become. Even if my story wasn't their favorite genre or style of writing, they could still try to see it through my eyes and give me helpful feedback.

The process of giving and receiving feedback is a key component of first-year writing courses, and learning to give praise is a part of it. The more you're able to go into this process with an open mind and try to see an author's vision for their paper, the better this experience will be for everyone involved.

IN CONVERSATION WITH THE WRITER

Feedback is fundamental to the writing process. Imagine you've just finished a first draft of an essay and are asked to turn in a second draft a week later. How would you know what to change? How would you know what to keep? Without receiving some feedback on your draft, you might feel like you're wandering through a dark cave, calling out for direction but only hearing your own voice bouncing off the rock walls. Feedback is another voice, a guiding voice, calling back to you to help you figure out that next step.

When giving praise or any form of feedback to a classmate, think about it as having a conversation. You're not grading their paper. You're speaking with them about how you are experiencing their work.

On the topic of praise, writing professor Ron DePeter (2020) said, "Meaningful praise...is feedback that recognizes something that is working for you as a reader, that gives you an opportunity to have a dialogue with the author, and that expresses some sort of appreciation for the work the writer has done, or for the writer herself" (p. 43). Note that DePeter uses the word "dialogue." When you write your margin notes[3] or your endnote[4] to the writer (or maybe you're filling out a rubric[5]), you're writing to them directly, letting them know how you're reacting to their work.

Praise is valuable in the revision process because it helps the writer know what parts to keep for their next draft and builds their confidence. In the following section, we'll look at how to give the praise in a way that's conversational and also specific.

HOW TO GIVE PRAISE

In first-year writing courses, you will be writing in different genres: personal narrative, rhetorical analysis, journalistic op-eds, and more. You may prefer one genre over another, in terms of reading and writing. Personal preferences are important to be aware of when giving feedback. For example, I really enjoy narratives, especially ones that use a lot of description and figurative language to bring scenes to life. I like to read between the lines to understand the author's meaning. You, on the other hand, may prefer argumentative papers that support the author's stance with research, facts, and data, presented in a clear and organized structure. The fact that we all have different reading and writing preferences is a good thing! Let's embrace it. When we read a classmate's paper, we will all react a little differently to it. What works for me may not work for you, and it's helpful for the author to see how multiple people are experiencing their writing. That's where you begin with feedback: by letting the author know what is working in your eyes. That's praise.

When you're giving praise to your partner, whether it's a note in the margins, in an endnote, or when filling out a rubric, you want to be as specific as possible. Simply saying, "I like this," "good job," or "great writing," isn't creating a productive conversation. The author doesn't know what exactly is working for you as a reader, and in the worst-case scenario, the author will think you're just rushing through your feedback and that you don't care to actually read their paper. The good news is that those short comments above can easily be expanded into meaningful feedback. For example:

- "I like the way you help us understand the main conflict in the first paragraph."
- "You do a good job of showing how the character feels and reacts in this moment."
- "Great writing. Each of your points in this paragraph is backed up by evidence and citations."

As you can see, the improved comments are much more specific about what exactly is working for you as the reader. Also, notice that the comments use "you" to speak directly to the author. Praise will boost the author's confidence, help them see how their audience is reacting, and let them know what techniques to continue to utilize in their writing.

---

3 Margin notes are comments you add to the paper as you read, typically in the margins (sides) of the paper. Most writing applications, such as Microsoft Word or Google Docs, will allow you to add comments to a text.
4 An endnote is a letter you write to the author. It can appear at the end of their paper or in a separate document. This is a letter that is addressed to the author, and you would use, "you," to speak directly to them. An endnote would include a combination of praise and constructive criticism.
5 A rubric typically contains the assignment success criteria and blank spaces to comment on whether or not the author has met them.

Let's look at a sample first paragraph from Nicholas's Literacy Narrative. This is a first draft. What praise would you give? One of my most memorable literary experiences I had was with my English teacher Mr. Venice in my third year of high school. It was the second time I've had him as an English teacher so he understood me more and helped me out a lot with my writing. The book we read that helped me the most and gave me the best memories was "Othello" by William Shakespeare. We read the whole book in the class together taking turns with each student in the classroom. All the chairs in the classroom formed a circle and Mr. Venice would pick students to be characters and read their parts. This made it more exciting as it seemed like we were the characters and gave us insight on the relationships between them and what they were plotting. This helped us get a basic understanding of the events and scenes occurring in the book but was far from close to the real action.

Examples of praise comments:
- "The way you describe how the chairs were formed in a circle helps me picture the classroom."
- "I like how you end on a cliffhanger. It makes me want to keep reading to get to the 'real action.'"

CONSTRUCTIVE CRITICISM

While praise is meant to help the author see what's working well, constructive criticism offers suggestions for what to change. Before you can jump in and give constructive criticism on a classmate's paper, you'll need to understand the "circumstances." As Straub said, "You're not just going to read a text. You're going to read a text within a certain context, a set of circumstances that accompany the writing and that you bring to your reading" (pp. 137-138). Consider the following:
- What is the assignment prompt? Reminding yourself of the assignment criteria can help frame your comments.
- At what stage in the writing process is the author? Is this a first or second draft? Is it a complete draft or a partial draft?
- How does the author feel about what they've written so far? Can you find out if the author has any specific concerns about their draft? Do you know what their goals are?

Typically, we don't do workshops to proofread a classmate's paper. Proofreading is the final part of the writing process, where you check over the grammar, punctuation, and spelling. While these finishing touches are important, they're not the primary concern in the early drafts. You want to think about the big changes first, such as whether or not the author has a controlling idea or if the paragraphs are in the right order. These big changes are referred to as "higher-order concerns." These "concerns are the big issues in the paper, ones that aren't addressed by proofreading or editing for grammar and word choice" (Gillespie & Lerner, 2008, p. 35). Professors Paula Gillespie and Neal Lerner (2008) offered a few questions to consider when dealing with higher-order concerns:
- Is the writer really addressing the assignment and fulfilling its terms?
- Is there a need for a thesis, and if so, is there one?
- Do arguments have the support they need? Is there an organization I can relate to as a reader? Is this piece addressing an audience in an effective way?

- Does the piece show appropriate levels of critical thinking? (p. 35)

By keeping these higher-order concerns in mind when reading your classmate's work, you can make them aware of larger issues. It might feel uncomfortable to point out these bigger concerns, but you're doing them a favor. Better to confront these issues sooner rather than later. In the next section, we'll look at the various ways to give constructive criticism comments.

TYPES OF CRITICISM

Below are three types of criticism. They can be used in margin notes, endnotes, or a rubric. They give you options for communicating potential areas of improvement to the author.

SUGGESTION

We want to refrain from telling the author they *need* to make a certain change. In the end, it's their paper, not ours, and they get to decide what direction to take it in. Instead, phrase your criticism in the form of a suggestion.
- "You could expand this scene by including some dialogue."
- "Your argument may benefit from adding more evidence in this paragraph."

QUESTIONS

You can offer suggestions in the form of questions. Maybe you'd like more clarity or for the author to expand on a certain part. Try forming your feedback as a question. The phrase, "is there an opportunity," can be helpful.
- "Where did this take place? Is there an opportunity to add more setting details?"
- "How specifically does the language of the article appeal to a young audience?"

PLAYBACK

Summarize a part of the writing. This helps the writer know how you interpreted it (Straub, 1999, p. 141).
- "It seems like you're saying your performance on the field got better as your relationship with the coach deteriorated. Are you sure this is the point you're trying to make? It seemed like you were saying the opposite earlier."
- "In your thesis, you summarize what the op-ed is about, but I'm not really seeing your own argument. What are you claiming about the rhetoric of the op-ed?"

PRAISE-CRITICISM CONNECTION

Let's return to the Straub (1999) quote from the beginning of this essay: "Be always of two (or three) minds about your response to the paper...Always be ready to praise. But always look to point to places that are not working well or that are not yet working as well as they might" (p. 140).

It's ideal to give criticism directly following praise. This way you've helped the author understand what's working well and where they might improve. These example comments include praise *and* criticism.

Chapter 7: Engaging Writers in a Dialogue of Revision

- "The topic sentence is strong in this paragraph. It relates directly back to your thesis statement. Is there an opportunity to connect the second example in this paragraph back to your topic sentence?"
- "I really enjoy the way you use smell to bring this space to life. Rather than summarize the conversation, I wonder if we could hear the characters' voices in dialogue."

Below is the second paragraph of Nicolas's first draft of the Literacy Narrative. What sort of praise-criticism comments would you give?

> Once we finished the book and had an understanding of the story and characters Mr. Venice put us in groups together for something big. He told us that he wanted each group to act out scenes from one of the acts from Othello using our understanding of the book. He assigned me and my group act 3 to film with each student being a character and recreating the scenes with the same idea but style. Since I was the director of all this I had to do all the writing for people's characters, scenes and possible props. We worked mainly in the wrestling room, which was a long and narrow dark red room with blue mat floors, black chairs, and some red soft objects. Since the room was dark we were able to have a gloomy look to our scenes, and act 3 also had a couple fights which we used the mats for. I would first write out a plan on how each scene would go and what I would use, then I would write out an explanation describing a character and give it to a student for them to study and finally film it.

Here are two examples of praise-criticism comments for Nicholas:

- "You help me understand the project when you say you were assigned to film Act 3 with each of your group members playing different characters. When you say, 'recreating the scenes with the same idea but style,' what do you mean by 'style?'"
- "It's interesting that you were the director. That sounds like an important role, and you make it clear that you had to do all of the writing. Help us understand how you came to be the director. Did your teacher assign you this role? How did it feel to take on such an important role?"

WHAT TO DO WITH FEEDBACK

After receiving comments from your peers or the professor, your goal is eventually to make changes to your paper that will strengthen it. However, it can be hard to know what to do when your paper is covered in marginal notes and you have an endnote from your reader with even more comments. In this section, I'll cover a few strategies for approaching revision.

It's important to read over all the feedback you received, but rather than just read it, take notes on the feedback. For example, you could reply to the marginal comments on your paper. Go through each comment and jot down your reaction to it. Do you understand it, agree with it, have questions about it? Jillian Grauman (2022), who has a Ph.D. in Rhetorical and Professional Communication, suggests you "mark any comments that you found confusing or you want to act on later. I also recommend keeping a list of things your reviewer noted that you did well—knowing your strengths is just as powerful as knowing where you can improve" (p. 155). In other words, react to the comments that you connect with and give you an idea of what to change. Also, take notes on the comments you're confused about; jotting down your reaction could help you process it. Remember, you can always follow up with your peers and teacher to ask for clarity. Lastly, Grauman makes the point that listing praise will help you see your strengths.

When it comes time to actually make the changes to your paper, I encourage you to think big. Return to the idea of the higher-order concerns. Do you need to work on your thesis statement or controlling idea? Is the order of your body paragraphs working and have you related those paragraphs back to your thesis? Does your conclusion pull together your main ideas and provide some takeaways? These are higher-order concerns. Consider returning to the assignment prompt and reading it over again. Did you meet the criteria? Professional writers aren't afraid to delete, rewrite, and add whole sections. Think about the people who have given you feedback. What types of revision would make their eyes light up and think, *wow, the writer really took my comments to heart!* Only after you address the higher-order concerns can you move onto lower-order concerns, which focus more on the sentence level, such as word choice, grammar, and in-text citations.

THE GROWTH MINDSET

You could encounter the situation where you receive a comment that makes you feel discouraged or question your ability. After all, you're taking a risk by allowing someone else to read your writing. Depending on the type of assignment, you could be sharing something personal, and criticism might trigger some negative emotions. In any sort of feedback situation, it's important to embrace the growth mindset.

The growth mindset is the belief that we can all improve our skills in any area with effort over time. It's the opposite of a fixed mindset, which is the belief that our abilities can't change, that we're either naturally good or bad at certain things (Dweck, 2016). One of the reasons I was so nervous to read my story aloud in that fiction writing class at Wesleyan University was because of how intimidated I felt by my classmates, by their beautiful prose and compelling stories. They seemed to have a natural ability for it, a talent that I simply didn't possess. This was my fixed mindset; they were born with talent and I wasn't. Yet, after I received some praise on my short story, I started to believe I could get better. I also learned that my classmates had previous experience with creative writing. They had put in effort over time to produce the type of stories I was envious of. With my newfound belief, I worked on making incremental progress by adopting the techniques that professional writers used. By the end of class, I wasn't churning out brilliant works of fiction, but I had developed a growth mindset and felt proud of my progress.

As Erin Kelly (2023), professor of academic writing, said, "When a comment knocks you back, you need to face it with a growth mindset – to see yourself both as someone who believes you can learn to revise your writing and as someone with the ability to think critically about what has come your way" (p. 308). If you get some harsh feedback and it triggers negative emotions, try to refrain from relating that comment to your overall writing abilities. Instead, view that comment as a growing opportunity. Try to separate your emotions from the writing and ask yourself, "what can I learn from this?" If you're confused about the comment or don't believe it has any merit, try reaching out to the person who wrote the comment for more clarity.

CONCLUSION

In your academic career, you may be asked to provide feedback in different formats. It could be a group workshop where you listen to a classmate read their work aloud, a peer review where you swap papers with a partner, or even a friend asking you to read their assignment for class. No matter the circumstance, if you remember to be of two minds—praise and criticism—you can feel confident that you'll enter into a productive conversation with the author and give quality feedback. Your unique reaction to the writing is valuable, and that's all you have to do: react and "wonder out loud with the writer about her ideas" (Straub, 1999, p. 137). Create a conversation through your comments and the writer will respond well. The writer is being vulnerable by sharing their work with you, and you can meet them halfway by using your authentic voice to show up and give them your best.

Don't skimp on yourself, either. Spend time reviewing and organizing the feedback you receive from classmates or the professor. Take notes on their comments, plan out your higher-order changes, and maintain a growth mindset as you approach your revisions. Writing is a skill. Giving feedback is a skill. Knowing what to do with the comments you receive is a skill. Each time you practice them, you get better, and the gains you make in this type of work will not only make you a stronger writer but also a better overall communicator.

DISCUSSION QUESTIONS AND ACTIVITIES

1. Have you had any experience doing a writing workshop or peer review? What was it like? What went well or didn't go so well?
2. Reflect on a time when you received helpful or unhelpful feedback on your writing. What made those comments good or bad?
3. What do you typically do when you receive feedback? What's your next step? Do you like your process or feel like there's room for improvement?
4. When it comes to your abilities as a writer, do you think you have a growth mindset or a fixed mindset? Why do you think that is?
5. Can you recall a time in your life (outside of writing) where you've adopted a growth mindset? What about a fixed mindset? What were the circumstances and how did this mindset impact you?

REFERENCES

DePeter, R. (2020). How to Write Meaningful Peer Response Praise. In D.L. Driscoll, M. Stewart & M. Vetter(Eds.), *Writing Spaces: Readings on Writing* Vol. 3) (pp. 40-51). Parlor Press. https://writingspaces.org/past-volumes/how-to-write-meaningful-peer-response-prais/
Dweck, C. S. (2016). *Mindset: The new psychology of success*. Ballantine Books.
Elbow, P. (1998). *Writing without teachers*. Oxford University Press.
Getchall, K. & Gonso, K. (2019). Valuing the process: Building a foundation for collaborative peer review. *Teaching English in the Two-Year College, 47*(1), 63–75. https://doi.org/10.58680/tetyc201930324

Gillespie, P. & Lerner, N. (2008). *The longman guide to peer tutoring* (2nd ed.). Pearson Longman.

Grauman, J. (2002). What's that supposed to mean? Using feedback on your writing. In D. Driscoll, M. Heise, M. Stewart & M. Vetter (Eds.), *Writing spaces: Reading on writing* (Vol. 4)(pp. 145-165). Parlor Press.

Kelly, E. E. (2003). The good, the bad, and the ugly of peer review. In T. Daniels-Lerberg, D.L.Driscoll, M. Stewart & M. A. Vetter (Eds.). *Writing spaces: Reading on writing* (Vol. 5)(pp. 299-317). Parlor Press.

Straub, R. (1999). Responding–really responding–to other students' writing. In W. Bishop (Ed.), *the Subject is Writing,* (2nd ed.) (pp. 136-146). Boynton/Cook Publishers.

CHAPTER 8

WRITING ACROSS THE UNIVERSITY

Alicia Clark-Barnes

CHAPTER OUTCOMES

- Apply writing processes from first-year writing to future experiences writing, studying, and working in college.
- Apply lessons from first-year writing to future experiences outside of academia.

KEY TERMS

- Introductory classes
- Writing-enhanced courses
- Writing resources

CHAPTER OVERVIEW

This chapter will address how to apply lessons from first-year writing to future experiences writing, studying, and working, in college and beyond.

BEYOND FIRST-YEAR WRITING

Imagine you are minutes away from answering the final question of your last final project before the semester break. You blink back exhaustion and keep pushing forward, and then, suddenly, you finish. As your shoulders sag and relief begins to wash over you, a friend appears and cheerfully greets you with, "Hey, looking forward to next semester?" Your brain stutters to a stop before you ruefully reply, "Sure, yeah, looking forward to it."

When you take a course with many components, like first-year writing, it can feel a bit like you have survived a writing marathon. There are short assignments, readings, videos, multiple drafts, conferences, and reflective writing to complete. You may feel palpable relief when you hand in that final assignment. And it is indeed an event worthy of celebration. But just as one successful project can lead to the next, the first-year writing course serves as an entryway to academic writing in college.

The thought of more writing may initially seem daunting or even torturous, but your first-year writing class has equipped you with strategies to tackle new assignments in other classes, and the habits you have worked so hard to build will serve you well in your classes and in your career. First-year writing was not easy, but you made it. Writing in any course is not easy, but you can do it. And there are steps you can take now to continue setting yourself up for success.

WRITING FOR INTRODUCTORY COURSES

After completing first-year writing, your likely next stop will be introductory courses in different fields of study. These courses are typically part of a general education curriculum, a series of courses designed to introduce you to different fields of study and ways of thinking. Introductory courses are designed for students who are new to the subject, so you may initially feel that these courses will be easy, but first impressions can be deceiving. As you start to read the first few pages of a new text, you may be surprised by how long the reading is taking you. There are a few new terms that you may pause to look up or highlight to return to later, and you may feel as if the sentences themselves are slowing you down. Where you are used to gliding along from point to point, it is now difficult to build momentum. This is normal. When you start a new hobby, you do not typically master it on the first try. Instead, you use what you have learned from other hobbies to improve. You observe experts. You get feedback on your approach. You practice over and over again. Here, we will apply strategies from first-year writing to an introductory course in another discipline.

READING

Your reading strategies may include finding the right physical space to complete the reading, a space with the amount of lighting and noise that allows you to focus. You may gather a laptop and headphones or notebook and highlighters so everything you need is at hand.

RHETORICAL SITUATION

When you begin reading a new text by first identifying the purpose the author is trying to accomplish and the strategies they use to connect with their audience, you are drawing upon the knowledge of the rhetorical situation that you practiced in first-year writing (See the chapter in this text on Rhetoric). You may find you instinctively respond to emotional appeals the author puts forth or recoil from an ethically questionable use of evidence. You may appreciate how a textbook transitions back and forth between examples and concepts or how a case study lays out the bare facts before drawing you into an individual's story. Your eyes and ears have become attuned to *how* the writer makes their point in addition to what that point is, and this analytical ability will help you break down complex arguments and allow you to weigh one set of facts against another.

NOTE-TAKING

In first-year writing, class sessions are typically discussion-based and the readings form the basis for class discussion. Readings may also serve as sources or models for the papers you submit. When taking notes on those readings, you needed a system to distinguish one reading from another while also leaving enough space for you to jot down your own viewpoint by including your reactions and highlighting what was most important to you about the style and content of the text. How did you decide where to enter the conversation taking place in the reading? How did you keep track of your questions along the way?

As you begin reading a new text, you may quickly skim through the entire reading first to get a feel for its structure and length and to decide what type of note-taking you should do to keep track of this new information. You may also think about what purpose this information will serve for you. Will you need to memorize key facts for an exam? Do you need to leave space for diagrams or problem sets to apply the concepts? Planning out your approach to readings and taking meticulous notes may make you feel like you are reading even slower than you were before. But in reality, you have taken on more responsibility for the material and are not only taking notes on what someone else has said, but are beginning to "write to learn." In "Writing as a Mode of Learning," Janet Emig (1977) connected the strategies we use to learn new information to attributes of writing. As you identify main points from the readings and organize your notes, you are using writing to process what you have learned from this new discipline. This seems simple because we have been taught to take notes from a young age but remember that you are selecting terms from an unfamiliar text and incorporating them into an organizational structure you designed in order to better understand these terms. If you have ever paused while taking notes to double-check your understanding of a term (or even your spelling), you can appreciate how writing helps to reinforce your learning.

PREWRITING, DRAFTING, CONFERENCING, AND PEER REVIEW

Your first-year writing class was probably smaller than the other general education classes you are taking. Your first-year writing instructor also likely broke down any writing assignments into smaller parts and included time in class for you to work on those parts. For example, you may have done an outline or brainstorming during class to prepare for a first draft, a draft which you received feedback on from your professor. You then wrote a second draft and received feedback from your peers. You also had the opportunity to read their takes on the assignment and to give them feedback. You incorporated this feedback and your own edits into a new draft which you proofread before submitting. After submitting, you reflected on what went well and didn't in the writing so that you could apply this knowledge to your next writing project. But the professor in your general education has not assigned any drafts and you do not receive time in class to work on the assignment. How does the process you learned in first-year writing apply to this class?

While the two courses may look very different, the greatest lesson you can take away from first-year writing is to remember how your writing process helped you to improve your papers. What was the best allocation of your labor? Maybe you get nervous attempting a new type of writing, but meeting with the professor individually allowed you to ask questions and inspired you to challenge yourself. You can still reach out to your professor over email or during office hours to ask questions about the assignment and to test out your ideas.

Maybe the knowledge that you were going to write multiple drafts made the first draft a little less stressful for you, because you knew you had more opportunities to work on the assignment. You can always write as many drafts for yourself as you would like, even if no one else reads them. How many times have you drafted a text and hesitated before sending it, then deleted it and wrote a new one before finally sending? No one will ever know how many drafts it took to get to the one you were satisfied with.

Maybe you found the opportunity to have 'another set of eyes' on your paper during peer review helped you to understand an outsider's perspective on your work. Or your partner's paper gave you new ideas for how to revise your own. You can still plan to exchange papers with a friend or classmate so that you can both benefit from more feedback and examples, even if your professor does not require this. Your friend can also hold you accountable, the same way a workout buddy can drag you out of bed to get to the gym and push you to race those last few feet. A writing buddy can help you ensure that you have given yourself enough time to get started on the paper or can talk through ideas with you if you get stuck. A writing buddy can also make the process more enjoyable, as you will have someone to complain to or laugh with along the way.

RESOURCES FOR WRITING

While many people find a writing buddy in their class, you may also find it helpful to write with or seek feedback from a roommate or fellow commuter, a teammate or partner, or a family member. While friends and family can provide wonderful support, if you are looking for feedback that is more impartial, a writing center is a space where students can work alongside tutors who are trained in how to give helpful feedback. These tutors have taken many of the same courses you will take, often with the same professors, so they can share strategies that they have used successfully. You can meet with these tutors in person or online, alone or in groups with friends. It can also be nice to speak with a trained person who is not grading your paper or with someone who has experience with a wide variety of approaches to writing.

A writing center might sound like a place to visit for English classes, but they are spaces, designed for writers working on any subject. You may attend for the first time with your whole history class to get feedback on your thesis statement. While in the center, you observe a student practicing a presentation while a tutor asks questions about the student's slides. Next to them, two students engrossed in an assignment prompt for a long project are discussing the best options for getting started. A student stops in with a quick question about a citation for their literature review while another student is meeting their group in the center to work on a business proposal. A writing center can also be a space to think and write at your own pace, in the company of other writers who can commiserate as you struggle to meet a word count or cheer you on when you discover the perfect ending to wrap up an argument.

WRITING IN THE DISCIPLINES

"I thought I did everything right, but I got a bad grade."

While many of the lessons from first-year writing can apply directly to another course, a paper for a writing class is not the same as a paper for a philosophy or history class, even though the requirements may be similar. This is because each academic discipline adheres to unique conventions of writing. You may have experience with using MLA to cite sources in an English class, but your Psychology professor will require you to use APA. You are still citing information, but you will use the citation style that best communicates the information most important to that discipline. While you will always continue to need evidence to support your points, the types of evidence used will also depend on the discipline. In a biology class, the evidence used could come from data collected during experiments, while in a sociology class, your evidence could come from interviews and observations (Cullick & Zawacki, 2016). In the following example, I explain mistakes I

Chapter 8: Writing Across the University

made writing my first paper for an intro to philosophy course.

In high school I was fascinated by transcendentalism so I was excited for my first college philosophy course, Philosophy of Being. For our first paper, we needed to respond to a question and support our response with course readings and outside sources. This seemed like a straightforward assignment. I defined one of my terms using the dictionary and when I got my paper back, the professor had written in the margin that I should have used a dictionary of philosophy and that I needed to be more precise with my arguments. I stayed after class to ask where to find a dictionary of philosophy. My professor explained that it was in the reference section of the library. When I looked up my term, I realized this dictionary explained the history of thinking about a word, rather than giving a few options for what a word meant. In using the nonspecialized dictionary definition, I was ignoring the evolution of the term and the implications of that evolution.

From that first philosophy paper, I learned that I would have to think abstractly but that philosophers were also highly disciplined in their thinking. The big ideas that I was so excited about were built upon dozens of tiny connections. In my writing, I would need to acknowledge those connections and to arrange my sentences with mathematical precision. Words like "if" and "then" could be the turning point of a whole line of thinking. I was frustrated by these restrictions and the way this style of writing forced me to slow down. But I also learned to pay more attention to both my writing and my patterns of thinking.

While writing for philosophy required the traditional essay format, writing in other courses may also look dramatically different. Amy Cicchino (2024) traced the experience of students in an introductory science course who were required to create scientific posters, a format typically used by scientists to share results in a professional setting. A student, Angel, who received an A in first-year writing, was dismayed to receive a C- on the poster. Angel met with the professor and learned why the essay writing approach she took, which included completing homework and classwork, creating an outline, citing sources in MLA, and adding a visual, did not translate to a scientific poster format. Her professor explained that Angel instead needed to create "a presentation of findings and data using relevant graphs or images, an evaluation of methods and processes, and specific recommendations based on data" (Cicchino, 2024, p. 169). Angel is initially humbled that utilizing successful strategies from English class was not the correct approach for a scientific poster. But she now understands that the purpose of creating a scientific poster is different from the purpose of writing an essay. Accordingly, her rhetorical decisions for science writing will be informed by how to evaluate evidence like a scientist and how to present evidence appropriately.

LEARNING AND RE-LEARNING

While you might already have learned the lesson of seeking guidance from a quality source and of matching your methods of thinking and writing to the subject you are writing about, this commitment to following the writing conventions of a subject is a lesson I have learned and re-learned many times. As a junior, after having completed the majority of my introductory courses, my political science professor stopped me after class to ask, with annoyance, why I had not written my paper about vice presidents in chronological order. I was embarrassed to tell him that I had subconsciously defaulted to searching for common themes across the leaders, an approach I often used in English papers. While either approach could be feasible, by not following a linear timeline, I had inadvertently distorted the historical context for some of my points, which was understandably a major error in the course. I may have covered the correct topics, met the page requirement, and cited my sources accurately, but I was not writing or thinking like a historian.

Struggling with a new type of writing can be a humbling experience and you may find you need to ask for help understanding a new style of thinking. When you take an introductory course, you are at the beginning of learning the terms and methods to think in a new way, much like when you learn the vocabulary, grammar, and culture of a foreign language. Managing the new information may be difficult, but your experience may also inspire you to take more courses in a discipline. Introductory courses are also designed to gently stretch your thinking and may allow you to see your old ways of thinking in a new light.

WRITING IN THE DISCIPLINES: DEVELOPING EXPERTISE

In addition to general education classes, you may eagerly await the opportunity to take courses in your major. This is the material you have been looking forward to and that you enjoy talking and thinking about. But as you take more advanced courses in your major, the expectations placed on you increase as well. You will be expected to understand more sophisticated texts and to apply knowledge from previous courses to new situations. Where you once read textbooks, now you must read articles and books written for insiders in your field. These texts may skip over explanations of terminology or practices because they are common knowledge for experts, but because you are still developing your expertise, you may need to consult an expert to fully understand why a finding is significant or why one type of evidence is more valuable than another.

Writing in your major can be exciting as your expertise begins to grow, but it is also full of challenges. As writing in the disciplines expert Dan Melzer (2011) noted: "Don't be surprised if you take a step backwards in your writing as you learn the conventions of writing in your major." Applying the rules and patterns for your field to your own writing is complicated because you are transitioning from student to creator of new knowledge within your discipline. You may also discover gaps in knowledge, places where your field has not yet solved a problem. As you prepare to help your field progress and grow, you will want to utilize the writing conventions that will demonstrate your new expertise and that will put your insights into respectful conversation with the wisdom of the past.

WHAT TO DO WHEN THE WRITING IS HARD

We would like writing to feel easier as we gain more experience, in the same way that you can make your favorite snack on autopilot because you have done it so often. But because each writing experience corresponds to a new rhetorical situation, it can feel like you are not making any progress as a writer. This feeling was even documented in a famous study from 1987 about one student writing for different courses. The author Lucille Parkinson McCarthy noted that the student-focused "so fully on the particular new ways of thinking and writing in each setting that commonalities with previous writing were obscured for him" (p. 137). But it is these commonalities that will help you when you encounter familiar challenges in new assignments.

What did you do in your first-year writing class when you did not understand part of the assignment? What steps did you take to break down a dense journal article into more digestible components? How did you determine when you had sufficiently analyzed a quote? How did you check that you cited a passage accurately? When your draft needed to be 500 words but you only had 300, where did you find inspiration? When you had too much to say, where did you start cutting out points? You may find that new and complicated writing problems require new and complicated solutions, but you may also find that past strategies will serve you well.

THERE ARE NO PAPERS DUE FOR MY CLASS

It may seem obvious that lessons from first-year writing can help you to write a paper in an introductory or Writing-Enhanced course or that you will return to those strategies for your capstone projects, but they come in handy in other areas as well.

There are many courses that do not require any papers. But do they require presentations? Or discussion posts? Or an essay or short answer questions on the exam? Will you create a final video or podcast to sum up what you have learned? Will you need to map your points onto a poster, complete with graphs and references, or translate nutrition facts to a blog post for elementary school parents? Do you need to write a proof to accompany your calculations?

As you transition from student to professional, how many drafts of resumes and cover letters will you work through? Will you craft a business plan or consolidate your findings into an executive summary? Will you evaluate current best practices and synthesize them into a curriculum? Will you draft a policy brief for an elected official? Will you email a parent about a sensitive subject or gently break bad news to a patient? Will you bring an audience to tears with your screenplay or lyrics? Will your poem echo softly across an auditorium?

Surely these projects demand the same attention to detail and commitment to process as any paper you have written. In your first-year writing class, you have the opportunity to practice and grow in your reading, writing, thinking, and listening. You will draw upon these skills in countless classes, but you will use them in your daily existence as well as you read attentively, write with care, think critically, and listen thoughtfully. Whatever you write next, may you always have the confidence that you have the words and the rhetorical knowledge to make a meaningful contribution.

DISCUSSION QUESTIONS AND ACTIVITIES

1. What genres are you now familiar with after taking first-year writing?
2. What specific writing strategies have you developed?
3. What new writing expectations do you anticipate in your other courses?
4. What writing strategies do you believe will translate from first-year writing to these courses?
5. Where can you find writing support when encountering difficult assignments?

REFERENCES

Cicchino, A. (2024) "I passed first-year writing—What Now?" Adapting strategies from first-year writing to writing in the disciplines. In T. Daniels-Lerberg, D. Driscoll, M.K. Stewart & M. Vetter (Eds.), *Writing Spaces* (pp. 168-188). WAC Clearinghouse. https://writingspaces.org/writing-spaces-volume-5/

Cullick, J. & Zawacki, T.M. (2016). *Writing in the disciplines: Advice and models.* Bedford St. Martin's.

Emig, J. (1977). Writing as a mode of learning." *College Composition and Communication,* 28(2), 122-128.

Melzer, D. (2011). *Exploring college writing: Reading, writing, and researching across the curriculum.* Equinox.

Parkinson McCarthy, L. (1987). A stranger in strange lands: A college student Writing across the curriculum. *Research in the Teaching of English.* 21(3), 233-265.

SECTION TWO:
WRITING PROJECTS

CHAPTER 9
COURSE INTRODUCTION: WRITING AND ASSESSMENT

CHAPTER OUTCOMES
- Demonstrate a basic understanding of course structure and processes.
- Examine and explain labor-based grading.
- Engage in a writing community.
- Practice generative and reflective writing.
- Reflect on prior writing experiences/contexts.

GETTING STARTED

The chapter focuses attention on introductory skills needed for academic success: Reviewing the course syllabus and objectives, as well as any guidelines and policies, for any course is a good idea. Another good habit to develop is checking your email and course announcements regularly. The chapter is also designed to slowly unpack how the first-year writing course operates and why it does so in that manner. Our goal as a program is not to rush you into an assignment but rather to explain the nuance, pace, and movement of the semester ahead.

This introductory chapter also concerns itself with you, the writer. In the early stage of the class, you will reflect on your previous writing/educational experiences and be introduced to the course objectives, alternative grading guidelines, and activities that support your entry into a new writing community. Some questions to consider early in the semester are: What have been your past writing experiences in and outside of school? What have been your experiences with feedback and grading as it relates to your writing?

PROCESS OVERVIEW

As we move into the sections that discuss the course writing projects, you will have the opportunity to explore and employ a variety of writing practices. Each of the writing projects includes an arc of assignments that focus on idea generation, drafting, workshopping, and reflecting. Writing is a collaborative and iterative process.

Introduction to Genre ⇒ idea generation and pre-drafting activities ⇒ draft 1 and writer's notes ⇒ instructor feedback conference and revision plan ⇒ draft 2 and writer's notes ⇒ peer feedback workshop and revision plan ⇒ final draft and project reflection.

DISCUSSION BOARDS AND REFLECTIVE WRITING

You are likely familiar with the concept of drafts, an ongoing process of writing and revision. What may be less well known are low-stakes writing assignments, times in which you will think through a new idea and/or consider your previous thoughts. This writing is less formal, so you can focus on content without being concerned with grammar and syntax. Although sentence-level concerns are something we will address as a class through the draft process, low-stakes writing is about idea generation.

DISCUSSION BOARD GENRE

Discussion board assignments are a common genre in a college setting. They are student-directed conversations that allow for multiple perspectives and ideas. Outside of the classroom in an online forum, you will have the time and space to post and respond thoughtfully. Here, you will write to learn about new topics and ideas in a low-stakes environment. Discussion boards provide an opportunity for you to begin to figure things out by putting your initial thoughts into words and interacting with your peers.

REFLECTION GENRE

To review, reflective writing is a typical writing assignment across courses and disciplines in college courses. Effective reflection includes a cycle where learners reflect before, during, and after writing. Reflective writing is integrated throughout the writing process, as it helps writers deepen their learning. With the cycle of reflection, you will look back at your prior skills and knowledge, consider choices within your writing process, and critically reflect on transferring what you have learned beyond the course. In your class, reflection can take on many forms, such as short in-class reflections, journal reflections that accompany your drafts, and robust reflections that occur at the end of the unit and semester.

STUDENT-CENTERED GRADING

Entering first-year college writing classes you may have only had experience with what we would consider to be traditional assessment, which, in many cases, is error-obsessed and final product-focused. For the better part of your careers, writing has been scored by a rubric, an approach to grading and instructor feedback that is overwhelming, imprecise, and constraining. Traditional numerical rubrics reduce instruction to a one-size-fits-all dynamic in which only students who meet the highest of standards are considered successful, leaving those writers who fall short of such expectations to develop increased anxiety and, as Kohn (2011) has noted, reduced motivation and work quality. When writing instruction values product over process, a particular student becomes the ideal, one whose voice, style, and register are said to be academic, code in many instances for white and middle-class, a point Inoue (2022) has made clear, that traditional grading practices lead to and uphold inequitable teaching and learning dynamics that do not value language diversity.

Assessment, however, should be inclusive, focused on meeting each student where they stand as learners. Instructors who apply a process-writing pedagogy emphasize individual growth through collaborative practices. To meet this mandate, we have developed an alternative approach to grading that is built from several assessment models, including labor-based grades, specification grading, and ungrading to support you and your growth as a writer and as a member of our writing community. Labor-based grading criteria values your efforts and labor no matter your writing experiences and/or perceived levels of success (Inoue, 2022). Specification grading connects your labor to the specific project and course learning objectives (Nilson, 2015). Ungrading puts the emphasis on the learning processes rather than the letter grade (Kohn, 2020). Through the combination of these assessment models, we aim to support and empower you to take ownership of your writing and learning.

Time spent working (labor) is the basis of course grades. While the act of writing is a central part of your grade (the time-labor dynamic), time reading, thinking, preparing, revising, and editing are also part of the time-labor equation. Your effort shouldn't be endless. Instead, your time and effort are linked to course credits. According to the Department of Education (2011), a credit hour is the unit of measurement used to indicate the amount of learning time required to achieve learning outcomes. Higher education institutions utilize the Carnegie Unit as the commonly accepted practice for the labor time associated with credit hours to include the time allotted in and out of class to meet objectives (The Carnegie Foundation for the Advancement of Teaching, 2007).

For each college credit, you can expect 2 hours of assigned work outside of classroom time. For example, for a 3-credit class, you will complete approximately 6 hours of outside class labor each week. Of course, some assignments may require you to use much or all of the provided time, while other tasks may take less time. Your labor in this class is not rote; it's purposeful. Labor aligns with your growth and centers on your learning. While the goals of each unit are to cross the finish line, the grading system values your efforts within the process, from understanding the genre, generating ideas, drafting, and giving and receiving feedback.

Final Grades Sample 3 credit course Total labor hours in class: 37.5 Total labor hours outside of class: 75	
A	Between 68 and 75 hours of labor outside of the classroom.
B	Between 60 and 67 hours of labor outside of the classroom.
C	Between 52 and 59 hours of labor outside of the classroom.
D	Between 45 and 51 hours of labor outside of the classroom.
F	47 or fewer hours of labor outside of the classroom.
Total labor ÷ 75 hours = Final Grade	

Involving you in the assessment process aligns with your success, individual goal-setting, and self-awareness of the learning and writing process (Fluckinger, 2010). After each draft, conference, and workshop, you will complete a single-point rubric to determine areas of your writing that have been successful and aspects in need of revision. While a traditional numerical rubric emphasizes scoring, a single-point rubric is a tool that is used for descriptive feedback, self-reflection, and revision planning (Fluckinger, 2010). Throughout the writing process, the single-point reflective rubric will be used as a self-assessment and collaborative tool between your instructor, your peers, and you to engage in a writing feedback dialogue. At the end of each unit, you will compose a project reflection of the unit that considers what you have learned and how you can apply that learning in other writing situations.

EXAMPLE

Single-Point Rubric: Draft 1 Writer Feedback		
Directions: Prior to conferencing with your instructor, review the criteria below that move from higher-order to lower-order concerns, as addressed above. Any criteria you feel has been addressed, please write "meets criteria" in the corresponding box.		
Project Criteria	**Writer's Notes**	**Instructor Feedback**
Criteria#1		
Criteria #2		
Criteria #3		
Criteria #4		
Criteria #5		
Criteria #6		
Revision Plan In a short paragraph, explain the specific revisions you plan to make and what outcomes you hope to achieve by doing this work.		

REFERENCES

The Carnegie Foundation for the Advancement of Teaching. (2007). The Carnegie Unit: What is it? The State University of New York. https://system.suny.edu/media/suny/content-assets/documents/faculty-senate/ugrad/TheCarnegieUnit.pdf

Fluckiger, J. (2010). Single Point Rubric: A Tool for Responsible Student Self-Assessment.. Teacher Education Faculty Publications, 5. https://digitalcommons.unomaha.edu/tedfacpub/5

Inoue, Asao B. (2022). Labor-Based Grading Contracts: Building Equity and Inclusion in the Compassionate Writing Classroom, 2nd ed. The WAC Clearinghouse; University Press of Colorado. https://doi.org/10.37514/PER-B.2022.1824

Kohn, A. (2011). The case against grades. Educational Leadership, 69(3), pp. 28-33.https://www.alfiekohn.org/article/case-grades/

Kohn, A. (2020). Forward. In S. D. Blum (1st Edition), Ungrading (pp. xxii-xix). West Virginia University Press.

Nilson, L. (2015). *Specific grading: Restoring rigor, motivating students, and saving faculty time*. Routledge.

United States Department of Education. (2011. May 18). Guidance to institutions and accrediting agencies regarding a credit hour as defined in the final regulations published on October 29, 2010. Department of Education. https://fsapartners.ed.gov/sites/default/files/attachments/dpcletters/GEN1106.pdf

CHAPTER 10
LANGUAGE AND IDENTITY

LEARNING OBJECTIVES:
- Introduce classroom guiding documents and practices and the alignment with ARE pedagogy.
- Foster a compassionate writing community where students will have opportunities to consider and critically reflect upon the intersection of identity, power, and language.
- Apply knowledge gained as they transition to examining language intersecting their identity and discourse community values (unit 1 discourse community narrative).
- Understand how ethnographic writing throughout this course allows us to analyze communities.

SECTION 1: EQUITABLE ASSESSMENT

In the first section of Unit 1, you will consider your previous experiences with writing assessment and learn about our student-centered approach to grading that values process over product, challenges language values and norms, and allows students to express themselves through language that is authentic to their lived experiences and sense of identity.

Chapter 11 focuses on the following:
- Writing goals.
- Writing growth.
- Writing assessment practices.
- Membership in a writing community.

DISCUSSION BOARD ASSIGNMENT

Following class discussions and reviewing content provided in the digital companion, please draft a discussion board post that addresses the following questions:
- What aspects of Inoue and Kohn's articles resonated with you and why?
- How might our class structure and grading policy align with Dweck's points about learning?
- What are your thoughts about our grading process? How can it benefit you? Our class community? What questions or concerns do you have?

SECTION 2: LANGUAGE AND IDENTITY

Understanding the politics of power associated with language is central to this course. In the assignment that follows, you will consider the relationship between language and identity. To do so, you will interrogate socially constructed concepts such as "standard" and "academic" English to understand better how these modifiers create and uphold hierarchies of language that privilege some and marginalize others. In the following unit, you will review literacy narratives that address these topics in preparation for your own writing.

After reading the provided texts in the digital reader, respond to one of the questions below.

In a 250-word response, refer to the text (paragraphs or direct quotes) and develop your response to include your experiences and/or connections to the question.
1. What have you learned about the relationship between language, identity, and power?
2. What are the issues associated with assigning Standard English modifiers like "normal," "proper," and "correct?"
3. What assumptions are made around language, dialect, and/or accents?
4. How does language provide access to some and deny it for others?
5. How can we value linguistic diversity?

DISCUSSION BOARD ASSIGNMENT - LANGUAGE AND IDENTITY

Please draft a discussion board post that addresses the following questions:
- What aspects of Inoue and Kohn's articles resonated with you and why?
- How might our class structure and grading policy align with Dweck's points about learning?
- What are your thoughts about our grading process? How can it benefit you? Our class community? What questions or concerns do you have?

OPENING WRITER'S REFLECTION

Building on your discussion board posts and classroom discussions about writing and our alternative approach to grading, write a 250-500 word opening writer's reflection.
- Articulate who you are as a writer thus far (up until this class), including relevant experiences and influences that have informed your ideas about being a writer and what constitutes "good" writing.
- Reflect on how our alternative grading method might impact you toward your own growth as a writer.
- Consider how community-based, collaborative writing supports your personal success as a writer and the success of your classmates. In other words, what will you and your classmates gain from approaching writing as a social practice?

REFLECTING ON PRIOR WRITING EXPERIENCES:
- How would you define a writer?
- What is "good" writing?
- How do these definitions apply to you?
- Where do you most often write? In what contexts? To what audience?
- What do you most often write about?
- What process do you follow when you write?

REFLECTING ON TRADITIONAL AND ALTERNATIVE GRADING:

- How do our alternative grading methods compare to your prior experiences being graded on your writing assignments?
- How may our student-centered grading approach to teaching and learning benefit you as a writer and member of our writing classroom community?

LOOKING AHEAD AND YOUR GOALS:

- What are your personal writing goals for the semester?
- What are your goals as a member of a writing community?

AUDIENCE: YOUR INSTRUCTOR

FAQ: Can I go beyond the word limit? Yes! Can I be creative and write this in a diary or letter format? Yes!

CHAPTER 11

LITERACY NARRATIVE: THE STORY OF YOUR UNDERSTANDING

Dana Jaye Cadman

CHAPTER OVERVIEW

Everyone has their own story. All stories are valid, but what is yours? How does your own relationship to reading and writing inform who you are? And how does this story connect to others? This essay on the Literacy Narrative form examines how a writer might use the facts of their lives, how they might select and curate and collect them and display them, and then discover and create a shape to them, to uncover and to share not only their individual stories but to connect them to the universal experience we all share of looking for meaning and understanding.

WHAT IS A LITERACY NARRATIVE?

Your teacher will ask you to write a literacy narrative. They'll show you what it is. And what it is not. A Literacy Narrative is a narrative essay they'll say, not a story. Not a story story. An essay story. A place for you to reflect and make meaning.

Maybe you'll be asked to read some examples, to figure out what they are. Your teacher might show you the classics: "Learning to Read and Write" by Frederick Douglass, "On Keeping a Notebook" by Joan Didion, "The Joy of Reading and Writing: Superman and Me" by Sherman Alexie, Malcolm X's "Learning to Read," Amy Tan's "Mother Tongue."

Or they might direct you to the DALN, the Digital Archive of Literacy Narratives, and ask you to browse. They might ask you to reflect on literacy itself, on what it means to you, and to society. They might explain: "The literacy narrative remains a popular assignment in writing classrooms, primarily because it encourages critical reflection on the diverse roles of reading, writing, and literacy on identity, literacy practice, and literate beliefs." (Alexander).

Here, your teacher will remind you that everyone has their own story, saying something about the validity of all stories, all modes of speech. "As the DALN is open access and digitally available worldwide, it provides a potential space for subversion of the grand narrative of the literacy myth through little narratives from people across a wide spectrum of literacy and cultural backgrounds, experiences, and ideologies." (Bryson). So your teacher will invite you to try.

Your teacher will probably ask, what was it like for you to first read? First write? Your teacher will tell you the story of when they first connected to books. Late at night, with a flashlight under their covers, lost in a story until dawn. And that is why they ended up as writing teachers. Don't you see? Your relationship to reading and writing informs who you are. You are sculpted by it. By the materials of your first books, your first journals.

The literacy narrative examines what you want to know. How you came about learning it. How you've entered the conversation. What did you read? Look up on the internet? Obsess about? What did that look like? What did you first create? What or how do you play?

AND WHAT IS THE POINT?

Sometimes we think the facts of our life are random and meaningless. And they are, in that it takes our own reflection, meditation, and interrogation to make sense and order and idea. It is the process of the writing itself which allows us to make meaning.

You are allowed to make meaning of your own story. To connect to memory and wonder why. To ask your reader to ask why.

But this is not a persuasive essay for a reason. You are sharing your story because it is inherently significant. You don't have to make an argument for that.

It is the sharing itself that validates your writing. You don't need a logical or rhetorical proof for the value of your individual story and voice.

But this doesn't mean there isn't a meaning. You and your life and your writing and your memory and thinking have meaning on their own.

However, as a writer, you select what to show, how to curate and collect it into a something take-in-able. So your reader can have their own moment of understanding.

You create a frame around a thought, a meaning. And that allows you to deliver something to your reader. You give them a chance to witness your experience and to wonder alongside you. To share in your revelations of content and form.

So when you build the structure of your literacy narrative, consider the classical shapes of the story.

THE SHAPE OF A STORY

Stories often open with an orientation into their setting. When you watch a movie, it might give you a drone shot showing the bird's eye view of a town. And then it zooms in, showing you the house of the protagonist. Then up close on their hands as they pour coffee.

Try that. Open your literacy narrative with where you are. What is the place you live? Your family of origin?

In a story, we'll see the everyday life first. What does it look like before the protagonist has to change?

Then we see the inciting incident. Thing-thing-that-happens. A storm rolls in. A new person moves to town. A plane crash.

In a literacy narrative, this is an encounter with a piece of literature. It might be a book. An article. A poem. A car. A horse. A backflip. It is a thing of intrigue. Something that makes you, the main character, wonder about the world.

Now that this thing has happened, the protagonist can not be the same. It wakes them, you, up to something beyond. This incident, this phenomenon or thing, creates curiosity. A wanting to know. And it sets you on a journey. A path to understanding.

So you create a shape, a structure, a cell that holds the machinery. You create a string of scenes that show this journey.

SCENE AND MEANING

You tell your story in scene. When we write scene, we create a place for meaning to be witnessed.

It's not that you won't explain the point in the literacy narrative, it's that the point becomes a real point in space. Scene is a set of concrete things. A moment in a world. Your world. So that the meaning you make in your literacy narrative has an anchor. A real, fixed thing to watch and look on and adore and understand. Something observable.

So we write our memories. Not our recollection of them but a way for the reader to watch them.

We let our reader see us going to the library as a kid and taking out a book on horses. Searching through social media feeds for experts on DIY haircuts. A book fair. Writing in our first diary or a letter to a crush.

When we mine our lives for stories, we can find the vivid things that stand out in sensual details. These unveil themselves and can be turned into meaning.

Why do you think you noticed the light on that day walking into a library for the first time? The way it fell on the street into the puddles. How did you feel while you were looking at it? Were you scared or moved when you first chose your own book to read? Did you choose it by the cover? Description? Just because it was lying around?

When I was eight years old I stayed up reading O. Henry stories. My dad had a volume of them on the shelf. The kind of set of books that adults place out in the open for their prettiness. They were cloth-covered in an emerald green color, and the edges of the paper were gold. They looked like treasures. I was a kid, so I probably didn't understand most of what the stories were about. But I read them, choosing each next one by perusing the table of contents for cool-sounding titles. I had the top bunk, or maybe by then my sister and I had already split rooms. I can't remember that part. But I know I was up too late with a reading light because I remember being alone. It was just me and the people in the stories. That was how I came upon "The Last Leaf." So when one person in the story does a beautiful, meaningful, kind thing for the other person in the story, and it turned out everything was meaningless after all, and maybe that's all life is, being beautiful and kind and meaningless for each other, I cried. I was a kid but I still got it enough to cry.

It was the first time a story I'd read had brought me to and through tears. I felt the experience I had witnessed, as much as I could understand it, and I cried with the people in the story, and maybe for everyone. I realized then the power of writing to help heal humanity.

That's one of my literacy narratives. There are the plays I wrote for my siblings, and the first lyrics I memorized, and the poem that won the contest, and the chat forums on the 90s internet, and the paper I got a D on, and the time I wouldn't get credit on my third grade reading log for a book about vampires because anything too weird or scary didn't count.

There are others, which are less directly about books or even words. There are the moments of unlocking just about anything. Of understanding coming into being. Watching a documentary on cheerleading and then getting lost in a historical internet search rabbit hole. The convention about snakes. The first website you built. When you figured out your style. The hours of videos you watched on making delicate macarons. That time you made a board game. The encyclopedic knowledge you possess of fictional characters inside of your favorite fantasy world. The way you can identify a car by its sound or identify a houseplant by the waxiness of its leaf.

HOW DO I CHOOSE?

What do you love?

When you first found that thing, you looked long at it. You investigated it. You adored it so much you learned its every corner and flaw. You wanted to add to it, to make things because of it, you thought about it and tried to figure it out.

You know those moments of knowing within that journey? When you break through to a new level in a game, when you make that final bendy rhyme at the end of a poem, when you learn a new fact, land a new trick?

Those moments are the scenes of witness. The experiences of literacies, when you come to understand the discipline you're learning. That's the unlocking.

Choose a memory or a series of memories that show a key, or a set of keys, in understanding the great mysteries of yourself, of knowledge, of life.

Literacy narratives show moments when our keys turn and unlock, when we open into new knowing or creation.

What was a time you came to understand something?

Remember as a child how it felt to build a sandcastle out of blocks? We play with the materials of sand or wood, come to understand the physics of it, and it fails and falls over and over again. Then, after trying. After watching it come apart enough, we come to understand how it is made. Then we can make one.

You ran to point out the castle. The way the tide came in and filled the moat just as you wanted, finally.

HOW DO I MAKE MY LIFE A STORY?

It already is. The literacy narrative allows you to write about your experience in the shape of a story rather than a persuasive essay. Your life does not exist to make a proof of it. Your life is a beautiful, meandering series of experiences and the meanings you make of them. That is why your life, your philosophies and your literacies, can be told in narrative.

Think about the ways you connect to and understand the protagonist in a novel or the main character in a movie. You watch the small moments, their reactions to them. You see what they see, what they focus on. Through this co-experiencing of life with them, you learn alongside them. When things happen to them, they happen to you, too.

So when you show your reader what your individual literacy narrative is, you are, showing them the story of your understanding.

The story of your understanding is the story of all of us.

Your experience, your beliefs, your intuitions, memories, background, youth, your voice—they are a significant piece in the shared story of humanity. Your understanding, your way of reading and writing the world, helps us all get closer to a complex and nuanced knowing. You help unlock the mystery that is all knowledge.

So your literacy narrative needs to be nothing other than your individual story. A moment within it, a single or series of scenes which describe an experience where you took in information and then/or created it.

When you consider what you know, what you understand, you can only, beautifully, offer your life. What is your story? How have you come to unlock the great mystery of understanding?

DISCUSSION QUESTIONS AND ACTIVITIES

1. Why might it be of value to consider and share your own stories of reading and writing?
2. What good comes from reading or listening to your classmates' experiences as readers and writers?
3. Share a literacy experience related to your time as a student with a classmate.
4. Share a literacy experience unrelated to school with a classmate.
5. How has language impacted your literacy experiences? For example, dialects, standard American English, and/or perhaps other languages spoken at home or heritage.

REFERENCES

Alexander, K. P. (2023). Reconceptualizing literacy: Experimentation and play in audio literacy narratives. Computers and Composition, 69, 102790–102790. https://doi.org/10.1016/j.compcom.2023.102790

Bryson, K. (2012). The Literacy Myth in the Digital Archive of Literacy Narratives. Computers and Composition, 29(3), 254–268. https://doi.org/10.1016/j.compcom.2012.06.001

CHAPTER 12
LITERACY NARRATIVE PROJECT

ENG 110 introduces students to ways of thinking about and using language to meet academic writing standards and expectations. The literacy narrative situates you and your experiences as a reader and writer as the first step in your exploration of and entrance into this new community of learners. The literacy narrative project starts with you.

HOW TO READ ASSIGNMENT PROMPTS

Before drafting or even beginning to brainstorm, you must first understand the nuance of the assignment. Too often, students jump in only aware of its general nature and not understanding its intricacy. When a student skips this critical first step, they often turn in work that does not meet the expectations of the assignment, which results in receiving no credit for their efforts, regardless of how good the writing may be.

Similar to other sections of this text, we recommend asking yourself some questions in preparation for writing:
- What is the general purpose of the assignment?
- What specific topic(s) has the instructor asked me to address?
- Is there an organizational pattern your instructor has requested?
- What steps or requirements has the instructor established? To answer this question, we suggest highlighting the assignment's action verbs.
- What genre am I expected to write in for this assignment?
  - How is this genre organized?
  - Does the genre require a thesis statement?
  - What forms of evidence are related to this genre?
  - What are the style and tone expectations associated with this genre?
- How many words or pages are required?
- How many sources should be included (if any)?

LEARNING OUTCOMES:

- Describe detailed literacy experiences in the writer's life.
- Analyze and interpret prior literacy experiences.
- Apply genre conventions and writing process.
- Create a framework for semester-long discussions of reading and writing.

INTRODUCTION

Literacy is the ability to read and write. Reading and writing, composing and communicating, however, happen in a myriad of ways. Your literacy journey may have begun at home or in the classroom. A book might have saved your life. A teacher may have presented you with a text that changed the way you saw yourself or others. Reading may have been a shared experience, a form of escape, or a chore you disliked. Writing may have been learned and practiced in solitude, telling stories, some real and others imagined, in the pages of a journal, for your eyes only, or a public act scripted over social media that artfully included emojis, slang, and acronyms.

PROMPT

In this assignment, you will write a compelling narrative essay in which you share a literacy experience (or a sequence of experiences) and explain the significance through analysis and critical reflection. Using narrative essay techniques, you will consider how these experiences have shaped, changed, and impacted how you understand yourself as a reader and/or writer. Narrative essays examine the significance of shared stories rather than only recounting them. They require writers to develop a controlling idea (a clear purpose for writing), articulate and analyze related experiences, and critically reflect upon these events to distill meaning. Writing a personal narrative essay is an opportunity to express yourself to an audience about the importance of your experiences. Being able to convey stories to specific audiences is a critical skill to develop for personal, professional, and academic contexts.

To find your focus, pinpoint specific moments of reading and writing which have left a lasting impact on you, such as:

- A vivid, early memory of reading and/or writing.
- A classroom experience, such as a time when reading or writing was challenging and/or transformative.
- A teacher who influenced your reading or writing journey.
- A favorite or specific genre in which you enjoy reading or writing.
- A time when written words helped you express yourself effectively.
- A book that shifted your perspective or changed your worldview.
- A piece of writing you are proud of and why.
- A page in a book, a poem, or lyrics that resonated with you and influenced the way you think about writing.
- A moment when a specific aspect of language shaped the way you interpreted a book you read or influenced something you wrote.

PROJECT CRITERIA

- Identify a personal literacy experience(s) of significance.
- Compose a narrative essay to include:
  - A clear controlling idea.
  - Effective storytelling techniques:
    - A narrative arc with scenes that capture key literacy moments.
    - Vivid details.
  - Essay genre conventions:
  - Analysis of specific experiences throughout the essay.
  - A critical reflection (a conclusion) as to how these experiences have shaped, changed, and impacted how you understand yourself as a reader and/or writer.
  - Style, tone, and syntax in consideration of your audience.
- Engage in the writing process throughout the project, including drafts, workshops, and conferences.

- Meet assignment expectations in response to the prompt, word count, format:
  - 750 words minimum, double-spaced, Calibri typeface, 12-point font, 1" margins).
  - Style, tone, language, and other writing conventions are appropriate to purpose, audience, and genre.

AUDIENCE
- Your peers and instructor.

DRAFTING SEQUENCE
- Review the assignment to highlight its specific guidelines and expectations.
- Genre Awareness, Generative, and Pre-draft Writing Workshops
- 1st Draft
- 1st Draft Writer's Reflective Rubric
- 1st Draft Instructor Conference and Post Conference Revision Plan
- 2nd Draft
- 2nd Draft Writer's Reflective Rubric
- Peer Conference and Post Conference Revision Plan
- Final Draft
- Project Reflection

USING THE WRITING CENTER

While you can use the Writing Center during any point of the brainstorming and writing process, in past semesters, writers working on this assignment have found it helpful to have sessions about:
- Brainstorming possible themes or controlling idea.
- Ensuring experiences are specific and meaningful.
- Ensuring experiences are analyzed and not simply recounted.
- Generating more in-depth insight into writing a critical conclusion.
- Organizing, sequencing, bridging, and transitioning between stages of the narrative.

GENRE AWARENESS AND EXPECTATIONS

Literacy narrative essays, a subgenre of personal narrative essays, follow the same conventions as good storytelling and include:

- A character – that's you! In your literacy narrative, you are the character. Your ability to turn yourself into a character by sharing information about yourself through your voice, identity, and experiences engages the reader. Remember, the audience doesn't know you. Provide ample information to help the reader gain an understanding of who is writing the essay, and unique aspects of yourself that help the reader get to know you (Lopate, 2013). For example, Matthew, a commuting college freshman, wears a yellow ski cap year-round (even in the summer) and likes to read and writes in a library near his home in suburban Westchester every Sunday. Now, those are great surface details; we can imagine Matthew, sort of. To get into the quirks of his character and how these nuances interact with his story, Matthew can show his character-in-action. Matthew might add that there were no other available seats at the library, so he crouched down to sit in a toddler-sized chair with his knees pressed up against the children's table reading and highlighting Meditations by Marcus Aurelius while being surrounded by toddlers flipping through books of his youth, such as those written by Patricia Polacco, Rosemary Wells, and his favorite, Mo Willems. These nuanced details provide insight into the character beyond the surface.

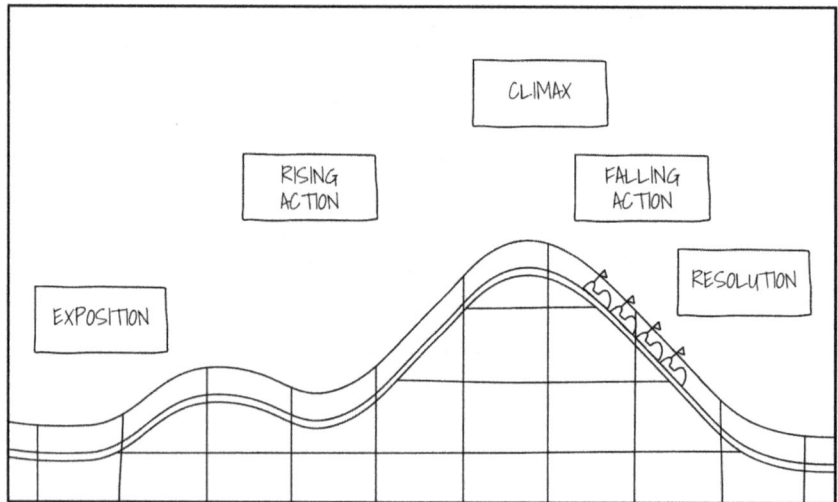

- A narrative arc includes a beginning, middle, and end. A narrative arc is what creates the plot and how the sequence of experiences progresses towards the end. Scenes build a narrative arc towards the total meaning of your experiences. The way your literacy narrative progresses does not have to be chronological, although chronological storytelling is the most common. You might sequence your literacy narrative chronologically, or you may start at the end and move backward in time, or you might start in medias res (in the middle) and move forward and backwards in time. When developing the sequence of your narrative arc, consider its logical progression, audience, and purpose. Matthew's next scene, for example, could be a toddler pulling off his ski cap.

Specificity in the experience shared. It helps the reader engage with your story. Specificity is reached by including the following:
- Setting
- Vivid details, such as sensory details
- Anecdotes and/or snippets of dialogue

The provided professional and student samples in this text and in the digital companion serve as opportunities to examine when and how writers add specificity to their texts.
- Conflict. A conflict is the main issue that the writer is trying to figure out. Conflict usually draws from the friction between what the character (that's you) desires in the outside world and their internal thoughts and feelings. Let's get back to Matthew's situation: he desires to complete the reading and assigned homework, but the conflict arises in the inability to find a quiet place to read and write, even in the library. This conflict becomes apparent in the scenes he chooses to narrate. Matthew's conflict unfolds through the selected scenes as he seeks to resolve the conflict. In the last scene, Matthew's cap was pulled off. In the first scene, it was noisy and his favorite books from his youth surrounded him. These scenes show the conflict escalating: Matthew needs to read and write, and he is distracted.
- Analysis and critical reflection. Analysis and critical reflection are essay conventions. Analysis allows a writer to guide the reader through the meanings of specific experiences. A critical reflection is the conclusion, which shows the significance of the total combined experiences, such as an underlying theme, which may be inferred or explicitly stated throughout the narrative.

GENRE AWARENESS EXERCISE

As reviewed in Chapter Five, genre awareness is the ability to recognize specific writing conventions and rhetorical strategies. The questions below guide you to rhetorically read the selected essays to determine and evaluate the choices made by the writer in that genre. Per your instructor's selection, review the selected text(s) in the digital reader.

Literacy Narrative Essays
- Where does the writer address language and identity in their essay?
- Where does the writer reflect on their experiences?
- What does the writer learn from their shared experiences?

Character
- What is the character's central conflict? Where do you learn this information?
- What do we know about the character? Where do we learn this information?

Narrative Arc
- How many experiences/scenes are in the essays?

- What is the order of the experiences? Chronological? Or starting in the middle or end? What is the effect of the order?
- What is the setting?

Specificity
- How many settings are in each essay? Highlight where the writer specifies a scene.
- Highlight where the writer uses vivid sensory details. Why did the writer choose to use vivid details in the specific area of the text? What effects do these techniques have on the reader?
- Do the writers use dialogue? If so, what effect does this have on the reader?

A controlling idea and/or main conflict
- Where do the writers indicate that the focus is around literacy?
- What is the writer's main conflict? Is it inferred or explicit?
- Where does the writer analyze or comment on their experiences?
- Analysis:
  - Highlight the sentence or set of sentences where the writer analyzes their experiences.
  - How does this analysis contribute to the controlling idea or conflict around literacy?
- Critical Reflection:
  - What do the writers learn about themselves through their literacy experiences?
  - Is there a deeper meaning inferred?

Audience
- How does the writer engage the reader through specific choices, like tone and word choice?
- What sentence or set of sentences is most engaging? Why?

IDEA GENERATION EXERCISE: HIERARCHY OF EXPERIENCES

1. Write down as many literacy experiences as possible in a five-minute speed writing round. These can be in no particular order and range from readings and writing to specific literacy skills, to events or persons that influenced your reading and/or writing life.
2. Circle the top three experiences that are significant to you.
3. Write a six-sentence story for each experience on your list.
4. Share your stories with your classmates and discuss which one is best to be developed into your literacy narrative. As an option, you may also consider how you might combine the stories from your list.

PRE-DRAFTING EXERCISE: FOCUSED FREEWRITE

Freewriting is a brainstorming technique that involves writing down whatever you are thinking about without stopping. You don't worry about spelling, grammar, or coherent sentences. And you don't need to worry about how messy your freewriting is, as the only one seeing your freewriting is you. A focused freewrite is when the period of time is spent trying to write as quickly as possible with a prompt in mind, such as the literacy narrative essay.

Chapter 12: Literacy Narrative Project

After selecting one of your stories or a combination of them in the previous activity, you will spend 10 minutes freewriting. If you are still stuck, summarize the experience or experiences in a few paragraphs or practice your narrative techniques, such as sensory writing and dialogue.

PRE-DRAFTING EXERCISE: SEQUENCING YOUR LITERACY NARRATIVE

This pre-drafting exercise challenges you to play and experiment with possible story sequencing. As you consider the shape of your essay, go back and review the literacy narrative examples that you read and discussed earlier in the project. What narrative structure do you plan to follow in your writing? Why do you think this structure is best for your story? After selecting your structure, use the visual organizer to sequence your literacy narrative and apply genre conventions.

VISUAL ORGANIZER

Category	Write
Narrative Scene #1 Establish the situation and introduce yourself as a character to your audience. Who are you? Where are you? Who are you with? When does this experience take place? What do you see, hear, smell, taste? What additional details will help your audience visualize the experience?	
Analysis What is the reason for including this scene? How does the scene relate to literacy? How does the scene support the larger purpose of your writing?	
Narrative Scene #2 Establish the situation and introduce yourself as a character to your audience. Who are you? Where are you? Who are you with? When does this experience take place? What do you see, hear, smell, taste? What additional details will help your audience visualize the experience?	
Analysis What is the reason for including this scene? How does the scene relate to literacy? How does the scene support the larger purpose of your writing?	

Narrative Scene #3 Establish the situation and introduce yourself as a character to your audience. Who are you? Where are you? Who are you with? When does this experience take place? What do you see, hear, smell, taste? What additional details will help your audience visualize the experience?	
Analysis What is the reason for including this scene? How does the scene relate to literacy? How does the scene support the larger purpose of your writing?	
Include more scenes and analysis as needed to develop your narrative in its entirety.	
Critical Reflection (conclusion only) What is the meaning of all of the shared experiences? How has the experience changed, shaped, and/or impacted you?	

At this stage of the project, you have completed the prewriting exercises and are now prepared to begin the drafting and feedback cycle.

Outside of writing your story, the drafting process also includes small reflective exercises: the reflective writer's rubric and conference revision plan. A reflective writer's rubric is submitted with your first draft and serves three purposes, all of which are meant to have the writer lead the discussion about their writing:

- Provides you the space to reflect on how you have addressed the prompt and assignment criteria.
- Directs your instructors and peers to the higher-order writing concerns you would like them to address.
- Explains why you believe these areas of your writing are in need of revision.

A conference revision plan is a short note that you write to yourself following your instructor and peer conferences. A conference revision plan serves two purposes:

- Offers an opportunity for you to revisit your draft and consider its strengths and what still needs to be developed and changed.
- Prompts you to prioritize the feedback into an order of importance that follows higher to lower order concerns.

Higher Order of Concerns (revision)	Meets Assignment Expectations Critical Focus, Thesis, or Question Organization Development Audience
Lower Order of Concerns (editing)	Style Word Choice Grammar Proofreading (spelling, punctuation, formatting)

PROJECT REFLECTION

CRITICAL REFLECTION

While you have reflected before and during the project to consider the changes to implement in your drafts, a critical reflection is an in-depth analysis of what you have learned and how that learning will apply to future writing contexts. Respond to one to two questions in each category below.

Looking Back
- What writing skills did you develop as a result of writing in the narrative genre?
- What aspect or aspects of the writing process were most helpful in developing your understanding and application of the narrative genre?
- What problems did you encounter while writing in this genre?

Looking Inward
- Where were you most successful in meeting the criteria of a narrative essay?
- What did writing a literacy narrative tell you about yourself and how you learn?
- How did the writing process inform you about how you learn and write?

Looking Outward
- What aspect of your writing would you want your audience to notice when reading your literacy narrative?
- What would your reader learn about you from looking at your writing?
- What's the one thing that you have seen in your classmates' work or process that you would like to try in your next piece?

Looking Forward
- What's one goal you would like to set for yourself when writing Project #2?
- What specific writing skills will you carry forward beyond the course?
- How could you be better supported as a writer by your classmates and/or instructor?

REFERENCES

Lopate. P. (2013). To Show and To Tell: The Craft of Literary Nonfiction. Free Press.

CHAPTER 13

UNDERSTANDING SOURCES THROUGH GENRE ANALYSIS

Jessica Kiebler

In this chapter, we will define genre and the ways that societal norms impact genre characteristics and usage. We will use the editorial genre to explore the process of genre analysis, which allows you, as a writer, to examine and interrogate the audience and rhetorical situation of sources. This chapter employs real-world scenarios to explain the importance of understanding genre to become a proficient writer, evaluate sources, and communicate effectively.

WHAT A GENRE CAN TELL YOU

Imagine that your friend asks you to go see a movie but you've never heard of the movie they want to see. You ask them what the movie is about to get some details. They respond that it is a documentary.

What information do you already have about that movie without asking any further questions? How would that information have changed if they said it was a horror movie? Or a comedy?

We can gather a lot of information on the content, format, and intended audience based on the movie's genre, which helps us make a decision about viewing it.

In the same way that movies use genre to communicate to viewers, writers use genre in similar ways through standards and conventions. These conventions allow readers to make selections, analyze texts, and make meaning from connections that exist across texts in a genre.

WHAT IS GENRE?

As you might recall from the essays in Section 1, a genre can be defined as a category of work, such as writing or film, that is characterized by specific style, format, and content.

Think about what characteristics might come to mind when your friend suggested watching a documentary:

- Non-fiction stories and information
- Usually made for the general public so it will include easy to understand content
- Educational content, perhaps even persuasive
- About the same length as a movie

These elements that relate to the format, content, and audience form the basis of the documentary film genre. Genres of writing might include poetry, literary narrative, biography, or editorial. These genre groupings and their related conventions allow us to identify sources, evaluate them, and select the most appropriate ones for our needs.

However, that definition has been expanded to show genre as "an ideologically active and historically changing force in the production and reception of texts, meanings, and social actions" (Bawarshi & Reiff, 2010, p. 213). The first definition only considers genre as a way to categorize information, while the second considers the social reasons and impacts behind those classifications. In other words, how do the genre categories and elements communicate to the reader about society? A newspaper article's purpose is to inform the reader about current events, while an op-ed/editorial is designed to sway the reader's opinion towards a certain perspective. The distinctive conventions of those two genres communicate their different purposes to the reader.

According to scholar Carolyn Miller (1984), genres are "typified social action" (p. 151). This means that as people write in similar situations and for similar purposes, the same elements are repeatedly used by others to help communicate effectively to an audience. And as new communication methods are introduced, such as social media, then genres may change or emerge as people adapt their communications. Think about the way you learned to format a tweet. The different styles emerging on TikTok like dancing or BookTok videos. The emergence of rap and hip hop as styles.

How do you better understand the conventions of a specific genre and how that impacts the message to the reader? That process is called genre analysis.

By identifying and analyzing the aspects of different genres, writers are better equipped to use those conventions in their own writing to effectively communicate with readers. For example, journalists are taught the structure, outline, and purpose for writing news articles in order to replicate those expected formats in their own pieces. Readers will then see those conventions, be aware they are reading news stories, and have a consistent experience across news publications.

WHAT IS A GENRE ANALYSIS?

Let's revisit movies for a moment. Movie criticism is a popular form of discourse in which content creators view, critique, and analyze films. Part of that analysis includes comparing them to other films within their genre to look for ways that the film is communicating with the audience. As writers, genre analysis is a similar method that builds awareness of the conventions within a specific genre, not only as a way to identify them but also to use them yourself. Devitt et al. (2004) explained that genre analysis identifies writing conventions and rhetorical strategies used by members of distinct communities to effectively communicate. You learned about rhetoric in earlier essays and that it can be defined as the study of writing effectively. And that the rhetorical situation is the context in which that communication occurs. This includes the author, setting, intended audience, the work's purpose, and the structure of the content.

In your upcoming assignment, you will analyze the editorial genre by looking at several examples to determine how conventions are considered across each editorial. For example, editorials have strong openings with a nuanced position (thesis statement), a mix of high-quality evidence (examples, data, research, experiences and connections to the topic), and a conclusion which furthers what the writer would like the reader to do, believe, or think after reading the editorial. Effective editorials make rhetorical decisions in consideration of their audience and purpose. By closely examining the organizational structures and rhetorical moves used by editorial writers, you will gain the skills needed to apply these conventions in your own writing and effectively engage your readers.

According to Bawarshi and Reiff (2010), "rhetorical situations, then, are social constructs, and genres are how we mutually construe or define situations as calling for certain actions" (p. 217).

What does this mean in everyday life?

If you need to let your professor know that you will not be in class tomorrow, how would you communicate that? Depending on the class rules, you would likely send them an email and write it in courteous, professional language. Let's look at this rhetorically. You are the author, writing to a person of authority in an academic setting with the purpose of expressing a specific message.

When you decide how to communicate with someone, you are performing a very small rhetorical analysis! You are considering the situation and content of what you need to express in order to match it with a compatible genre or format.

In academic settings and in your upcoming assignment, you will ask more detailed questions as you analyze editorials or opinion pieces for genre conventions and the rhetorical situation. Devitt et al. (2004) provided questions you should ask yourself:

- Where does this genre of writing take place?
- What topics, ideas, and content are communicated in the genre?
- For what purpose are these pieces written?
- Who is the intended audience of this genre?
- Who writes these works? Do they all share certain characteristics?

In addition to compiling information about sources within the genre, you will also judge the effectiveness of how the authors present their information and whether the writing is persuasive to you as the reader. You will consider how they use the genre's conventions to encourage you to act in some way based on the author's work. This will also prepare you to write your own editorial and apply the same writing strategies within that genre.

WHY ANALYZE EDITORIALS AND OPINION EDITORIALS?

In the upcoming unit, you will select and analyze writings from the editorials or opinion genre to complete a genre analysis.

Why are editorials a great choice for this analysis? Starting in the early 1880s, editorial articles were "in a newspaper, magazine, or similar publication that expresses the editor's opinion or the publication's position on a topical issue" (*Oxford English Dictionary*, para. 2). Even as many newspapers moved online, this tradition has continued and evolved.

Editorials are still written by a high-ranking journalist or the editor of the publication and have their own section. However, opinion editorials have also emerged as a genre which allows for more diverse perspectives and contributions to publications. They are usually published separately from both the editorials and the objective journalism on current events. Anyone can write opinion articles to express a perspective on a topic, whereas editorials are written solely by journalists and curated closely by the editor. Authors of opinion pieces are often experts or have a specific relationship with a topic, such as a resident in a town writing about a housing issue.

Editorials and opinion articles are a valuable genre to use for genre analysis because of the clear rhetorical situation and genre conventions.

Chapter 13: Genre Analysis

Think back to the movie example and the elements that identify a documentary. If someone asked you how to identify an editorial, could you give them specific elements to represent it?

Take a look at the chart below for some examples:

Rhetorical Situation	Editorial Genre Elements
Setting	writing takes place in a newspaper or magazine intended to inform/educate
Content	topics are usually related to current (potentially controversial) topics and issues
Purpose	authors intend to provide their viewpoint to persuade readers towards their ideas
Audience	can be the general public for publications like newspapers; or the audience can be within a specific discipline if the publication is a scholarly journal or magazine
Author	the author's relationship to the topic can impact the effectiveness of the message (For example, a teacher writing about the impact of AI in the classroom)

In your editorial genre analysis, you will take this concept a step further by not only looking for examples of rhetorical elements, but also editorial-specific genre conventions and evidence of the effectiveness of the writer's arguments.

It is important to recognize the genre conventions in your analysis because they are key elements that a reader expects when reading editorials. With each editorial, you will begin to see these recurring patterns in the structure of this form of writing. These conventions include things like the information included in each paragraph, the types of evidence used, the persuasive language methods, and how the writer considers the rhetorical situation.

For example, journalist Bryce Covert (2021) published an editorial about the return to work in a post-COVID world and how this is an opportunity to discuss the issues with current workplace expectations for hours and remote work. Covert used the genre convention of emotional language when crafting the title, "8 Hours a Day, 5 Days a Week Is Not Working for Us," hoping to resonate with readers who share that feeling. The article then starts with a strong thesis that we should be working less as a society (Covert, 2021). It continues with multiple paragraphs of evidence ranging from international studies on employee satisfaction to the health risks of overworking. The editorial ends with a reconnection back to the thesis that COVID policy removal should be a time to discuss how work impacts our lives.

By exploring the conventions of editorials, you will be able to apply the genre analysis process to other sources in order to identify and model those essential markers in your own writing.

GENRE IN EVERYDAY LIFE

You will have many opportunities to engage in genre analysis as you move through your personal and professional life. By studying the unique elements and conventions of different sources, you understand when and why you should use them (or not!) so you can more easily select the most appropriate sources for your needs.

You wouldn't use a Tweet as evidence in a professional report to your boss. Or send a scholarly research article to your mom who just asked for some background information on a topic.

When you understand sources more deeply, you are also able to evaluate sources more effectively. Genre and source analysis skills are incredibly valuable in a world of ever-expanding source types where authority is very unclear and based on the context of the information.

DISCUSSION QUESTIONS AND ACTIVITIES

1. In small groups, select a movie, song, or TV series. What's the genre? What specific elements (or conventions) help you recognize that genre? In small groups, list 2–4 key elements you noticed, and then identify another two movies, songs, or TV shows that share those same genre conventions.
2. Consider a piece of information you read for this class recently. What genre of writing does that work fall into? What elements or conventions help you recognize this genre? What patterns or conventions stand out to you? For example, what tone, language, or structure makes you recognize the genre?
3. Consider how you communicate every day on social platforms, by text, or through email. In small groups, create a short guide for one of these genres. For example, if your professor wanted to post on a class Instagram page, what conventions would you tell them to follow? What about a tweet? What would you tell them to avoid? Make a quick list of "Dos" and "Donts" for the genre you choose.

4. What strategies might you use when you are unfamiliar with a genre that you need to write?
5. What strategies might you use when searching online for editorials and opinion editorials? How would you determine which of your search results were editorials?

REFERENCES

Bawarshi, A. S. & Reiff, M.J. (2010). Genre: An introduction to history, theory, research, and pedagogy. Parlor Press; The WAC Clearinghouse. https://wac.colostate.edu/books/referenceguides/bawarshi-reiff

Covert, B. (2021, July 20). 8 hours a day, 5 days a week is not working for Us. New YorkTimes. https://www.nytimes.com/2021/07/20/opinion/covid-return-to-office.html

Devitt, A.J., Reiff, M.J., & Bawarshi, A. (2004). Scenes of writing: strategies for composing with genres. Pearson/Longman.

Miller, C. R. (1984). Genre as social action. *Quarterly Journal of Speech*, 70(2), 151–167.

CHAPTER 14

GENRE ANALYSIS PROJECT

LEARNING OUTCOMES:
- Demonstrate genre awareness.
- Describe key characteristics and conventions of the op-ed genre.
- Analyze op-eds to determine how their conventions and structure shape communication with a specific audience.
- Explain rhetorical choices made in this genre.
- Compose an analytical thesis and essay.

INTRODUCTION

Genre is a type of writing that is characterized by specific conventions, structures, and purposes. Writing in a genre requires an examination of how it functions to meet the needs of its audience. This is a genre analysis, a study of how genres are defined by their unique features and how these elements serve particular functions and audiences. By analyzing the features of a genre, genre analysis helps to uncover how different types of communication are constructed and interpreted within various fields or social settings.

This assignment is designed to help you gain familiarity with the opinion editorial genre, also known as an op-ed. An op-ed is a text that expresses a writer's opinion on a specific topic, issue, or current event. They are typically found in newspapers, magazines, and across digital platforms, such as Ted Talks and blogs. While op-eds are often written by experts, anyone with a unique perspective on an interesting topic can produce this writing. A compelling op-ed makes a clear argument to a specific audience by articulating the writer's connection to and perspective on a contemporary issue, providing specific, relevant examples, and including quality sources.

PROMPT:

Writing a genre analysis requires you to break from your previous writing instruction or natural inclination to construct an argumentative essay in which you agree or disagree with the authors or use the texts to present and support your own position on a selected topic. Your goal is to explain not what the authors are writing about but rather how they are writing about an issue by analyzing their use of structure, writing conventions, tone/style, and rhetorical strategies. Your essay should focus on the ways in which the writers accomplish their goals by using and adapting key genre features for their specific purposes and audiences.

Conducting a genre analysis is beneficial to you as a writer in a variety of ways:
- Understanding the conventions and expectations of a genre helps writers to effectively communicate in a manner that is appropriate for an audience.

Chapter 14: Genre Analysis Project

- Analyzing genres helps writers organize their content, choose appropriate language, apply rhetorical strategies, and use stylistic elements effectively to engage with an audience.
- Examining the underlying purposes of different genres helps writers understand how and why certain conventions are used, the effectiveness of their writerly choices, and what impact they have on an audience.

PROJECT CRITERIA

- Getting Started
  - Select three op-eds that address a single contemporary issue in education related to reading and/or writing.
  - Identify the rhetorical situation for each op-ed.
  - Examine the recurring features in the genre (structure/organizational pattern, evidence, rhetorical strategies, style/sentence structure/word choice/tone).
  - Compare how the writers adapt these genre conventions for their purposes and audiences.
  - Determine three genre features used by the authors that most effectively engage, communicate, inform, and/or persuade their audiences. These three features will serve as the focus of your essay.
- Compose a genre analysis essay to include:
- Introduction
  - Define genre analysis and explain its purpose.
  - Introduce the issue you selected to review and explain its personal and/or contemporary significance.
  - Provide the rhetorical situation for the op-eds reviewed (who is writing, for whom, the publication, and the purpose).
  - Include a thesis that states the three conventions you will analyze and why you selected these features.
- Analytical Body Paragraphs
  - Include two analytical body paragraphs for each genre feature (convention) mentioned in your thesis.
  - Each body paragraph should focus on one specific convention (e.g., structure/organizational pattern, evidence, rhetorical strategies, style/sentence structure/word choice/tone).
  - Begin each paragraph with a topic sentence that makes a clear genre analysis claim connected to your thesis.
  - Support your claims with specific, cited examples from the op-eds using MLA citation style.
  - Analyze how and why the selected convention is used effectively by the writer(s) to engage, inform, or persuade their intended audience. Focus on the writer's rhetorical choices and their impact on communication.
- Conclusion paragraph
  - Summarize the primary characteristics, conventions, and any significant patterns or trends you identified in the genre.

- Discuss the importance of your findings and how they contribute to a deeper understanding of the genre.
- Consider techniques learned from closely reviewing op-eds and what conventions you may adopt when developing an effective op-ed of your own.
- Engage in the writing process throughout the project, including drafts, workshops, and conferences.
- Meet assignment expectations in response to the prompt, word count, format:
  - 1000-1250 words minimum, double-spaced, Calibri typeface, 12-point font, 1" margins).
  - Style, tone, language, and other writing conventions are appropriate to purpose, audience, and genre.
  - MLA Citations

AUDIENCE

Your peers and instructor.

DRAFTING SEQUENCE

- Review the assignment to highlight its specific guidelines and expectations.
- Genre Awareness, Generative, and Pre-draft Writing Workshops
- 1st Draft
- 1st Draft Writer's Reflective Rubric
- 1st Draft Instructor Conference and Post Conference Revision Plan
- 2nd Draft
- 2nd Draft Writer's Reflective Rubric
- Peer Conference and Post Conference Revision Plan
- Final Draft
- Project Reflection

USING THE WRITING CENTER

While you can use the Writing Center during any point of the brainstorming and writing process, in past semesters, writers working on this assignment have found it helpful to have sessions about:
- Choosing essays that are at the appropriate level of writing and thinking;
- Ensuring genre analysis of sources is being applied rather than source summary;
- Identifying the audiences, evidence, rhetorical strategies;
- Developing an analytical thesis (usually occurs after you've read your selected pieces).

GENRE AWARENESS AND EXPECTATIONS: BUILDING AN AWARENESS OF THE GENRE OF GENRE ANALYSIS

At this point in the semester, you've already practiced examining the genres you write. In the literacy narrative unit, you learned how narratives follow specific conventions and

Chapter 14: Genre Analysis Project

from your close reads, you developed a set of skills to develop your literacy narrative in consideration of the genre. Building awareness of genre conventions benefits you not only in this course but across your classes. Since we won't cover every genre you will ever write, becoming an expert at understanding how to recognize genres and genre conventions through analysis is of great importance.

For example, early in my career at a television channel, my colleague asked me to provide feedback on a script and video rough draft of a television series episode. I needed to give detailed feedback to the producer, but I never watched the series, so I needed to familiarize myself with the genre's features to better understand the show's signature style, content, structure, and audience expectations. I spent hours reading multiple scripts, watching multiple episodes, and diagramming the patterns I noticed across the shows. By recognizing the key features across the episodes, I became aware of the specifics of the genre, which equipped me to give feedback to the producers.

In your academic, professional, and personal lives, you will surely write and communicate in many genres and for differing purposes and audiences. Your genre analysis project will teach you how to look closely at genres so that you can apply this practice throughout your academic and professional careers.

GENRE AWARENESS EXERCISE: WHAT DO WE KNOW ABOUT WRITING A GENRE ANALYSIS ESSAY?

As we've reviewed, genre awareness is the ability to recognize writing conventions that shape different genres. Reading student examples helps you see how writers (just like you) approached this project. When reviewing student examples, we read them just like reading professional work; we read rhetorically to pay attention to how writers adapt genre conventions for their specific purposes and audiences. The questions below will prompt your critical reading and guide your discussion about the choices the writers made.

Please review the selected student genre analysis essay in this text and/or the digital reader.

GUIDING DISCUSSION QUESTIONS:

1. Introduction
   - Where do they define genre analysis? Why might this matter for setting up the purpose of the essay?
   - Where does the writer introduce the rhetorical situations of the texts they analyzed?
   - Does the writer indicate the significance of the contemporary issue? How so?
   - What genre features does the essay focus on? Where does the writer make that clear?
2. Body Paragraphs
   - What features are analyzed?
   - What information is included in each body paragraph?
   - How is the information organized?
   - Does the writer support their analysis with evidence from the texts reviewed?
   - Does the writer support the analysis with explanation?

3. Conclusion
- What information is included in the conclusion paragraph?
- How does the conclusion help you understand what the writer learned about the op-ed genre?
4. Style/sentence structure/word choice/tone

With your partner or in a small group, read a paragraph or two out loud.
- Discuss how the writer engages with the audience.
- How would you describe the authenticity in their voice?

GENRE AWARENESS EXERCISE: WHAT DO YOU KNOW ABOUT OPINION EDITORIALS?

By the end of this activity, you should begin to understand the purpose of an op-ed and identify key features of the genre.

GUIDING DISCUSSION QUESTIONS:

- What do we know about opinion editorials?
- Who writes them?
- Where can you read, watch, or listen to an opinion editorial?

In pairs or small groups, look up the following:

- A definition of an opinion editorial (op-ed).
- A basic video review of rhetorical situations.
- An op-ed example (from the digital reader).

To gain awareness of the op-ed genre, we have adapted and added to the questions Devitt et al. (2004) provided:

- Where does this genre of writing take place? Where are op-eds published?
- What topics, ideas, and content are communicated in the genre?
- For what purpose are these pieces written?
- Who is the intended audience of this genre?
- Who writes op-eds?
- What are key features of the example op-ed?

Great. Now that you have some understanding of the genre, your instructor will assign you a cluster of op-eds to read before the next activity, which provides you a collaborative opportunity to work through the steps of writing a genre analysis.

GROUP GENRE ANALYSIS: VISUAL ORGANIZER ACTIVITY

As you've seen in your close reading of three op-eds, genre conventions are the shared features that signal one form of reading/writing from another. For example, readers are

Chapter 14: Genre Analysis Project

aware of the differences between an opinion editorial as opposed to a news report or a comic strip.

We should note that genres are not stagnant or rigid. While genres do have conventions and opinion editorial writers do work within constraints, genres are flexible. Writers are absolutely not robots; they bring themselves to their texts and use rhetorical strategies to adapt genre features for varying purposes, audiences, and contexts.

By the end of this activity, you should be able to:
- Determine the rhetorical situation for each op-ed.
- Identify and describe genre convention patterns seen across the texts.
- Analyze similarities and differences in conventions used.
- Determine the features you believe to be most effective in engaging the topic and audience.

Rhetorical Situation	Guiding Questions	Op-Ed #1	Op-ed #2	Op-ed #3
Author	Who is the author? What makes them credible?			
Topic	What is the topic of the op-ed?			
Context	What is the publication for each op-ed? What do we know about the publication?			
Purpose	What is the author's perspective? What does the author want the reader to do, believe, or think?			
Audience	Who is the readership and what does the readership value?			
Exigence	When was the op-ed written? Why was it socially, culturally, and/or politically important at that time to write this article?			

Conventions	Guiding Questions	Op-Ed #1	Op-Ed #2	Op-Ed #3
Structure/ Organizational Pattern	How does each writer organize their writing? In what ways does the organization guide the reader through the writer's claims?			
Evidence	What evidence is used across the genres (e.g., personal stories/ experiences, data, research, interviews)? Consider the balance of evidence. Does one writer rely heavily on one type of evidence? Why might that be? Why do the writers select and include specific types of evidence? Example: Op-Ed #1 integrates scientific studies to bolster claims about reading reform, whereas Op-Ed #2 uses a personal anecdote about their child's challenges with reading. Op-Ed #3 draws on classroom experience teaching the three-cueing method.			
Rhetorical Strategies	Does the writer attempt to connect with the audience emotionally? If so, how? How does the writer establish credibility and/or trust with the audience?			

Style/Sentence structure/Word choice/tone	What is the tone of each op-ed (formal, casual, funny, stern, etc)? Is the language more formal, informal, conversational, other? Why might that tone be effective for their authenticity? For the audience? Are the sentences mostly short? Or are they long? How does the sentence structure affect the connection between the writer and reader?			

MAKING SENSE OF THE VISUAL ORGANIZER: ANALYZING GENRE CONVENTIONS

Now that you've documented the rhetorical situations and identified patterns of conventions across the op-eds, you can now begin your genre analysis.

In your group, select three genre conventions that are most effectively adapted by the writers to meet their purpose and connect with their audiences. For each, discuss *how* the convention is used and *why* it is effective. You may choose to select examples from all of the op-eds or highlight just one or two.

While determining what conventions stand out, consider these guiding discussion questions:

- Which conventions (e.g., structure, evidence, tone, rhetorical appeals) stand out as most impactful?
- How do different writers adapt each convention to suit their purpose and audience?
- What makes these adaptations effective?

By the end of this activity, you should have:
- Selected three genre conventions.
- Noted specific examples from the op-eds.
- Explained how each convention works and why it matters.

Convention # 1 • What convention are you focusing on? • What evidence from the op-eds (either 1, 2, or all 3 op-eds) shows this convention as impactful? • Why is this choice effective for the intended audience and purpose?
Convention #2 • What convention are you focusing on? • What evidence from the op-eds (either 1, 2, or all 3 op-eds) shows this convention as impactful? • Why is this choice effective for the intended audience and purpose?
Convention #3 • What convention are you focusing on? • What evidence from the op-eds (either 1, 2, or all 3 op-eds) shows this convention as impactful? • Why is this choice effective for the intended audience and purpose?

Now that you've practiced a genre analysis as a group, you're ready to begin developing your own by applying the same strategies to your individual project.

Let's get started.

IDEA GENERATION: FOCUSED FREE-WRITE / PRE-LIBRARY WORKSHOP

With a clear understanding of a genre analysis, your first step is to research op-eds on a current issue in education related to reading and/or writing. In the upcoming library workshop, a librarian will guide you in locating relevant publications and finding op-eds through the Pace University database.

To prepare, take a few minutes to jot down ideas or do a focused free-write. What is a current issue in education related to reading or writing that matters to you?

Reflect on your personal experiences in education or any recent news or social media stories related to reading and writing that you find interesting, relevant, or even frustrating. Take five minutes to freewrite on the following:

- What educational issues interest you?
- What do you already know about them?
- What experiences have you had with them?
- What do others write or say about the issue(s)?
- What do you think?
- What do you wonder or want to learn more about?

You'll return to this freewrite when you begin searching for op-eds during the library workshop.

In your session you will find several links to popular sources and sources that include opinion editorials on educational issues.

PRE-DRAFT VISUAL ORGANIZER

Once you've selected your op-eds, follow the same steps you practiced in the group activity above. A copy of the same visual organizer has been added to the digital reader. You can use the organizer to begin mapping out the rhetorical situations, comparing op-ed features, and drafting your analysis. The organizer mirrors the format used during your practice activity, so the process should be familiar.

PRE-DRAFT OUTLINE

With your visual organizer complete, you're now ready to begin shaping your genre analysis essay. As you consider the genre and its conventions, use the insights and details from your organizer to help structure and develop your essay. The organizational pattern below will guide your approach. Think of the outline as a tool to experiment with the development and organization of your analysis. When writing in an unfamiliar genre, we find outlines can be especially helpful in working within the genre's basic structure.

Outlines provide a space to work out new ideas before writing a draft. It is informal/low-stakes writing. Below, you can find the assignment criteria to help guide your thinking. Use bullet points or include as much detail as you feel is necessary. Refer to the digital reader for a copy that you can populate.

Introduction Paragraph
- Define genre analysis and explain its purpose.
- Introduce the issue you selected to review and explain its personal and/or contemporary significance.
- Provide the rhetorical situation for the op-eds reviewed (who is writing, for whom, the publication, and the purpose).
- Develop a working thesis that includes three conventions you will analyze (e.g., structure, tone, types of evidence, rhetorical strategies) and how and why these conventions are impactful/effective for the given rhetorical situations.

Body Paragraphs
The bullets that follow are provided to help you get started. You should not write responses to each of them. Instead, review your visual organizer and develop analytical paragraphs around specific features. For example, you may write a paragraph about how the writers use evidence or how the writers build credibility with their audience. Your paragraphs should follow the organization developed in your thesis. You will write two body paragraphs for each claim made about the genre conventions.

The organization of each body paragraph is as follows:
- Include a clear topic sentence with a genre analysis claim aligned with the thesis.
- Provide examples of a specific feature such as structure, writing conventions, tone/style, or rhetorical strategies.
- Explain how and why certain conventions are used, the effectiveness of these choices, and what impact they have on an audience.

Conclusion
- Summarize the primary features/conventions and any significant patterns or trends you identified in the genre.
- Discuss the importance of your findings and how they contribute to a deeper understanding of the genre.
- Explain why the genre's characteristics are significant and how they affect the genre's purpose and audience.
- Consider strategies you might use or avoid when developing an effective op-ed.

DRAFTING SEQUENCE

At this stage of the project, you have completed the prewriting exercises and are now prepared to begin the drafting and feedback cycle. The drafting process mirrors the same one as the literacy narrative project, which includes drafts, small reflective exercises, instructor conferences, and feedback workshops. You may also choose to visit the writing center for individualized feedback from a writing consultant at any stage of the writing process.

PROJECT REFLECTION

CRITICAL REFLECTION

While you have reflected before and during the project to consider the changes to implement in your drafts, a critical reflection is an in-depth analysis of what you have learned and how that learning will apply to future writing contexts. Respond to one to two questions in each category below.

Looking Back
- What writing skills did you develop as a result of writing in the genre analysis genre?
- What aspect or aspects of the writing process were most helpful in developing your understanding and application of writing a genre analysis?
- What problems did you encounter while writing in this genre?

Looking Inward
- Where were you most successful in meeting the criteria of a genre analysis essay?
- What did writing a genre analysis tell you about yourself and how you learn?
- How did the writing process inform you about how you learn and write?
- How did the process help you understand the meaning of your writing?

Looking Outward
- What aspect of your writing would you want your audience to notice when reading your genre analysis?
- How did the process help you understand the meaning of your peers' essays?
- What would your reader learn about you from looking at your writing?
- What's the one thing that you have seen in your classmates' work or process that you would like to try in your next piece?

Chapter 14: Genre Analysis Project

Looking Forward
- What's one goal you would like to set for yourself when writing your op-ed (project #3)?
- What specific writing skills, attitudes, and behaviors will you carry forward beyond the course?
- How could you be better supported as a writer by your classmates and/or instructor?

CHAPTER 15
WRITING AN OPINION EDITORIAL
Shirli Sela-Levavi

CHAPTER OVERVIEW

This chapter discusses the function of opinion editorials in the age of the internet and social media. It explains the state of mind required to write an opinion editorial.

OPINION EDITORIALS AND THE PUBLIC SPHERE

You started your 110-course writing your personal literacy narrative and went on to develop your rhetorical skills by studying a specific genre, the opinion editorial. Now, you will be asked to write your editorial as a more skilled writer. This step marks not only a new intellectual challenge but also allows you to step out of college writing and into the public sphere.

The public sphere is an institutional location where debates take place to promote democratic ideals (Weisser, 2004, as cited in Kent & Couture, 2004). The necessity of debate and discussion for a healthy democracy was stressed by many prominent philosophers (Eckstrand, 2020). Important thinkers like Jurgen Habermas suggested that the public sphere is necessary in order to make people's needs heard by the authorities. The public sphere is a space where problems can be detected and voiced loud enough so that the government would feel the need to respond (as cited in Eckstrand, 2020). The editorial genre is one important tool for making the individual voice heard in the public sphere.

Rhetoric and speaking in the public sphere are historically intertwined, as the Greek orators and rhetors used to make their speeches in the central meeting place of the police, the agora. Later, after the invention of the printing press, newspapers became an important medium for public debates. The invention of the radio and television has contributed additional venues to public sphere discourses, whereas the emergence of the internet around 25 years ago and the development of social media have added a whole new dimension to the concept.

It is debatable whether the internet is conducive to democracy or whether the opposite is true. On the one hand, it offers people from all parts of society equal access to political debates since it is cheap and easy to use. On the other hand, lack of regulation and the abuse of the system by governments and individuals through algorithms for selective dissemination of content can be detrimental. In any case, in the 21st century, one cannot disregard it as an important arena for public conversations. The internet has greatly diversified the venues and opportunities for voicing opinions. Therefore, for you, as a student, it can be a great tool for intervening and influencing agendas that you care about. While publishing your opinion in a newspaper is difficult, publishing on the Internet is much more accessible. However, as Spiderman's father said before he died, with great power comes great responsibility.

PREPARING TO WRITE YOUR EDITORIAL

Now that you are about to make your voice heard in the public sphere, your challenge is threefold:

First, you must focus on an ongoing debate that you care about; it is not enough to be interested in it intellectually; usually, writers of opinion editorials have a stake in the topic they write about. Therefore, their writing is both argumentative and passionate.

Second, you must learn the history of the debate: What has been said on this topic so far and by whom? In what circumstances has this topic been debated? As you learned in the second unit, opinion editorials are either written by a newspaper's editorial board, by experienced journalists, or by experts on the topic. This is because an opinion editorial will be worth reading only if you have learned the facts very well before you formed your own opinion.

Third, you have to plan your own intervention in the ongoing debate. This does not mean that you have to form a yes/no opinion. Most debates are more complicated than that. For example, some proponents of gun control acknowledge people's right to protect themselves. Therefore, they argue that a person can carry a gun for self-protection but deny people's right to carry automatic weapons. Some people think that abortion should be allowed until the end of the first trimester but prohibited when pregnancy is more advanced.

SO, CAN I USE THE WORD "I"?

As a well-established genre, opinion editorials have a relatively fixed structure. Starting to write your editorial you must remember that this genre is argumentative in nature. This means that your unique voice must be heard throughout. Students often think that to make their voice heard, they should use the word "I" very often. This is only partly true. In fact, saying "I" too many times will render your writing more poetic and personal and less argumentative. Start arguing your point by relating to other opinions and situating yours within this context, and you will note that you can say many things that are clearly your opinion without saying "I" too many times.

YOUR VOICE GAINS AUTHORITY

If you have prepared for writing your editorial as suggested above, you deserve the right to be heard. Remember, however, that you will be heard as a knowledgeable, mature person who voices their opinion among other adults. You are no longer the student sitting in the classroom, nor the person who wrote papers, trying to satisfy certain academic requirements. Instead, imagine yourself sitting among peers who are your age or older. They will keep listening to you as long as your voice is sound and clear, as long as you do not use slurs and bad words, and as long as you make convincing arguments.

You can use ethos, but you do not have to quote. As this is a short genre, it is better to simply learn from other people's writing, but when you write your editorial, make their arguments your own and express them in your own words. This is not an academic genre, so you do not have to cite. You can use pathos to a reasonable degree, and, of course, you should use logos very deftly. Keep adhering to the genre's conventions as you learned in unit 2. You will not hear the audience applaud when you are done, but you might get readers' responses and comments. Be prepared to feel empowered.

DISCUSSION QUESTIONS AND ACTIVITIES:

1. Re read an opinion editorial on a topic that interests you. What motivates the author to write on/about the selected topic?
2. How does the author establish credibility with their reader?
3. What does the writer believe the audience knows or thinks about the topic?
4. What does the writer want the audience to do, believe, or think after reading the op-ed?
5. How does the writer use structure, rhetoric, style, and tone to connect with the audience?

REFERENCES

Eckstrand, N. (2020). Complexity, Diversity and the Role of the Public Sphere on the Internet. Philosophy and Social Criticism, 46(8), 961-984.https://philarchive.org/rec/ECKCDA-2

Weisser C.R. (2004). In B. Couture & T. Kent (Eds), The Private, the public, and the published: reconciling private lives and public rhetoric (pp.230-248). All USU Press Publications. https://digitalcommons.usu.edu/usupress_pubs/148

CHAPTER 16:
OPINION EDITORIAL PROJECT

LEARNING OUTCOMES:
- Apply op-ed genre conventions, adhering to genre-specific elements such as structure, tone, and audience considerations.
- Create a compelling argument with clear purpose that effectively engages and persuades readers.
- Use rhetorical strategies to engage and persuade readers.
- Demonstrate research that incorporates and synthesizes credible sources to support claims and enhance argument.

INTRODUCTION

As discussed in Unit 2, an op-ed is a text that expresses a writer's opinion on a specific topic, issue, or current event. They are typically found in newspapers, magazines, and across digital platforms, such as Ted Talks and blogs. While op-eds are often written by experts, anyone with a unique perspective on an interesting topic can produce this writing. A compelling op-ed makes a clear argument to a specific audience by articulating the writer's connection to and perspective on the topic, providing specific, relevant examples, and including quality sources.

PROMPT

Using the conventions learned in Unit 2, write a nuanced opinion editorial on a contemporary issue in education related to reading and/or writing. This can be the same topic you previously explored or a new one. The writing should relate to your own experiences and interests. Your op-ed should contribute to an existing conversation, be directed to a specific audience, and present a compelling argument that includes evidence to support your position. Writing should be clear, engaging, and persuasive and aim to influence public opinion, spark debate, or generate discussion.

PROJECT CRITERIA

- **Getting Started**
  - Select a timely and relevant topic that interests you about an educational issue related to reading and/or writing. This can be the same topic explored or a new one.
  - Conduct research.
  - Develop your purpose.

- **Determine your audience.**
  - Introduction
  - Include a lede.
  - Highlight your connection to the timely topic.
  - State your critical argument clearly, quickly, and concisely.

- **Body Paragraphs**
  - Develop a clear organization approach and sequence of ideas.
  - Incorporate relevant examples, facts, and statistics to support your argument.
  - Don't forget that this is about your opinion and experiences.

- **Conclusion**
  - Briefly revisit the main points or evidence.
  - Reinforce the urgency or importance of your argument.
  - Include a call to action or strong statement offering what you would like the audience to do, believe, or think about the topic.

- **Engage in the writing process throughout the project, including drafts, workshops, and conferences.**
  - Meet assignment expectations in response to the prompt, word count, format:
  - 650-800 words, double-spaced, Calibri typeface, 12-point font, 1" margins).
  - Style, tone, language, and other writing conventions are appropriate to purpose, audience, and genre.
  - MLA Citations

- **Audience**
  - First-Year Students.

DRAFTING SEQUENCE

- Review the assignment to highlight its specific guidelines and expectations.
- Generative and Pre-Draft Writing Workshops
- 1st Draft
- 1st Draft Writer's Reflective Rubric
- 1st Draft Instructor Conference and Post Conference Revision Plan
- 2nd Draft
- 2nd Draft Writer's Reflective Rubric
- Peer Conference and Post Conference Revision Plan
- Final Draft
- Project Reflection

USING THE WRITING CENTER

While you can use the Writing Center during any point of the brainstorming and writing process, in past semesters, writers working on this assignment have found it useful to have sessions about:

- Identifying an issue or topic that will allow you to address the assignment's requirements.
- Locating and/or synthesizing sources.
- Developing and organizing an argument.

OP-ED GENRE AWARENESS REMINDERS

In your genre analysis project, you developed skills to recognize how writers use and adapt genre conventions when writing op-eds. Now, it's your turn to apply those conventions in crafting your own.

We encourage you to return to your prior work where you have already explored issues and topics around education, reading, and writing. What was the issue of concern in your literacy narrative? Is that a meaningful topic in which you have an opinion or that you would like to learn more about? Or what about the op-eds that you reviewed for your genre analysis? Do you have an opinion about the issue explored? What about the classroom discussions and other texts read? You might consider topics from the review of your peer essays or perhaps an issue from Dr. Mundy's introduction or the essays that follow. As you are aware, writing op-eds requires a connection to the issue or topic. Be sure to select a topic that is meaningful to you.

As with the earlier projects, you'll engage in the writing process through a series of generative, pre-drafting, and drafting activities. The writing process for op-eds is especially recursive. Op-eds require you to learn about the issue and include quality research. The process truly mirrors this image:

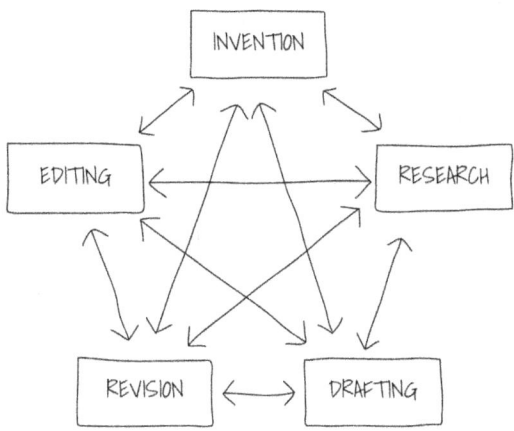

You discover a little. You do a little research. You develop your point of view. You go back and learn some more. You revise and refine your point of view. You learn some more. You consider how to best adapt genre features for your audience, purpose, and context. It's now the time to synthesize the skills and knowledge gained from the last project and apply them to writing your op-ed.

IDEA GENERATION: LIST MAKING

First, you'll need to identify an educational issue related to reading or writing that is meaningful to you. Take some time to make a list of topics of interest. To do so, review your prior work and topics explored in the semester.

- What issue was your literacy narrative about? Could it be an area of focus for your op-ed?
- What issue was the focus of your genre analysis? How could you address this topic from a new angle? What would your personal experiences add to this dialogue?
- What other contemporary issues related to education interest you? Which one or ones may be a good fit for an op-ed?

IDEA GENERATION: 10-MINUTE FREEWRITE

Review your list and spend 10 minutes free writing about an issue that stands out to you. Don't worry about too much of anything except writing. When we freewrite, we allow ourselves the freedom to think and not worry about what the end result looks like.

A freewrite allows you to riff and/or rant about the topic without stopping to worry about grammar, punctuation, structure, or spelling. Don't worry; your instructor won't collect or grade your freewrite. This is your space to simply write–to put words on the page, to explore and discover ideas and areas of writing interest. Remember, this activity is meant to be messy, so do not write with the goal of producing a polished draft. There will be time for that much later in the writing process.

Some guiding questions to help you get started:

- Why is this issue significant to you?
- What do you know about the issue?
- What personal stories or experiences do you have with this issue?
- What would you like other students to know or think about this issue?

IDEA GENERATION: INDEPENDENT LIBRARY RESEARCH/ GATHERING EVIDENCE

You've landed on a topic and identified why the issue matters to you. Now, you'll learn more about the topic by conducting library research. Through this process, you'll gather and identify quality sources and explore what others have said about your selected issue.

As you research, consider the following questions:
- What are other opinions about this issue? How might their perspectives challenge, support, or complicate your point of view?
- How have researchers studied the topic? What studies are significant? For example, if your topic is on closing the reading literacy gap in elementary schools, you might find a national study on the results of reading literacy.

To support this next step, you'll complete a short Library Wizard activity that will guide you through using academic databases and help you develop and refine your search strategies.

*Remember that drafting op-eds is not linear. You will most likely return to the library database to gain additional insight, clarify a concept, and include additional source material, all of which will refine your writing and strengthen your argument.

PRE-DRAFT ACTIVITY: PLANNING YOUR OP-ED

Now that you've explored a topic of interest through freewriting and library research, it's time to begin planning. This is not a formal outline but rather a pre-draft exercise designed to give you space to reflect on your perspective, clarify your position, and jot down ways you might support your stance using evidence and rhetorical strategies. Remember, this activity is not about being perfect; it's about getting your ideas down that you would like to build upon in your essay.
- Briefly describe the specific education/reading and/or writing issue you're focusing on.
- What experience do you have with this issue? Jot down your personal connection and experiences you have had or observed.
- What op-ed or research are you responding to or building on? Include the titles/authors/publishers.
- How have their perspectives aligned or differed from each other?
- How have their perspectives aligned or differed from your unique understanding of the issue?
- Why does this issue feel urgent or timely to write about now?

Your Position (Thesis)
- State your position in one clear sentence (10 words or less). As reviewed in your genre analysis, op-eds require the writer to state this quickly, clearly, and succinctly.

Supporting Points (Don't worry about paragraph structure yet—just note ideas). Remember, it's up to you to determine the way you use evidence. Although this is an opinion editorial, your experience and personal connection are essential. How you choose to use additional source material is determined by your purpose, audience, and context. We suggest a balance between personal experience and quality sources, which will provide you credibility as an engaged and knowledgeable author.

- Point 1:
  What evidence will you use to support this point?
- Point 2:
  What evidence will you use to support this point?
- Point 3:
  What evidence will you use to support this point?
- Additional Points:
  What evidence will you use to support this point?

Conclusion
- What do you want your reader to do, believe, or think differently after reading your op-ed? Why should they care? Why now?

RE-READING OP-EDS

As you develop your op-ed structure, it's a good idea to continue to read and reread the genre in which you will write. Re-reading rhetorically gives you the time to notice the writerly choices made: how writers structured their op-eds, using evidence, rhetorical strategies, and style to engage and persuade their audiences. In your re-reading consider techniques you might try in your own piece. For example, how did that writer hook the reader? How did that writer weave personal experience in or integrate quality research? What might you borrow from their approach?

PRE-DRAFT OUTLINE

At this point, you've clarified your position, identified your audience, and gathered your evidence. Now it's time to organize and structure your op-ed based on your goals and your audience's expectations. It's also time to consider your style, sentence structure, and tone. While it might be nice to have a one-size-fits-all template, an op-ed requires you, the writer, to make rhetorical choices for your purpose, audience, and context. How do you want to lead the reader through your opinion and argument? Where might you include personal experience or research-based evidence? What do you want your reader to walk away with/think about/do after reading your essay?

While we have provided you with a space with a skeleton structure, please adapt conventions to create an impactful op-ed for your readership. Your reader is an incoming first-year student, so what kind of structure, evidence, style, and tone will you use? What rhetorical strategies can be helpful in connecting you to your readers?

INTRODUCTION SECTION

As you develop your opening section, look closely at the rhetorical strategies of other op-eds you read. We are hesitant to state "write an opening paragraph only," as op-ed writers create compelling openings utilizing various rhetorical strategies. As you develop your opening section, look closely at the rhetorical strategies of other op-eds you read.

LEDE
What have other writers done to draw in the reader? Of those approaches, which will you incorporate into your writing?

CONTEXT
Why does this issue matter now? What is your connection to the topic?

YOUR OPINION/THESIS STATEMENT
Clearly state your main opinion or position on the topic. Be short and direct. Aim for 10 words or less.

BODY PARAGRAPHS: WHAT POINTS DO YOU WANT TO MAKE ABOUT THE ISSUE?
Each body paragraph should focus on one clear point and supporting evidence. Take note of how op-ed body paragraphs are structured, including length. Op-ed paragraphs are often shorter and more concise than the paragraphs you may be used to writing in academic settings. Rather than aiming for a set number of paragraphs, focus on articulating 3–4 distinct points to address that clarify and expand upon your thesis.

POINT #1, #2, #3, …#4
- Evidence or Example (experience, research, differing perspectives and opinions)
- Why it matters: Explain how this evidence supports your argument and helps the reader understand your position.

CONCLUSION
- Revisit your argument.
- Remind the reader why this issue matters now.
- Make Impact: What should your reader think, do, consider, or change as a result of reading your piece?

DRAFTING SEQUENCE
At this stage of the project, you have completed the prewriting exercises and are now prepared to begin the drafting and feedback cycle. The drafting process mirrors the same one as the literacy narrative and genre analysis projects. You may also choose to visit the writing center for individualized feedback from a writing consultant.

PROJECT REFLECTION
As you are aware from the prior projects, a critical reflection is an in-depth analysis of what you have learned and how that learning will apply to future writing contexts. Respond to one or two questions in each category below.

Looking Back
- What writing skills did you develop as a result of writing in the op-ed genre?
- What aspect or aspects of the writing process were most helpful in developing your understanding and application of the narrative genre?
- What problems did you encounter while writing in this genre?

Looking Inward
- Where were you most successful in meeting the criteria of an op-ed essay?
- How did the writing process inform you about how you learn and write?
- What did you learn about the power and value of your own experiences as they relate to larger social, cultural, and political issues/topics from writing the op-ed?

Looking Outward
- What aspect of your writing would you want your audience to notice when reading your op-ed essay?
- What would your reader learn about you from looking at your writing?
- What's the one aspect of writing that you have seen in your classmates' work that you would like to try in the future?

Looking Forward
- From this project, what specific writing skills will you carry forward beyond the course?

CHAPTER 17
CLOSING REFLECTION

As stated in Robert Mundy's introduction, "we ask our students to come as they are not as they have been told to be, to drop the pretense, avoid the posturing they have been taught, and engage with their professors and peers, along with themselves, openly, honestly, and genuinely". This closing reflection is your opportunity to look back and critically reflect on your experiences in this class. Before writing, please review the opening introductory chapter again.

In this closing, your final steps include:
Write a reflection of at least 250 words in length in response to the below questions and supported by evidence from your semester of writing.

WRITING OVERVIEW
- Who were you as a writer entering ENG 110?
- Who are you as a writer now that the course has ended?
- How do you see yourself evolving as a writer in the future?

TRACKING YOUR DEVELOPMENT
- How have you developed an authentic voice as a writer?
- How has this challenged your previous experiences with writing?
- How have your experiences in ENG 110 helped to shape the writer you are and want to be?
- What is one meaningful writing experience you've had this semester? Why did it stand out?
- How did working through a writing process contribute to meaningful writing?

LEARNING OUTCOMES
Provide an excerpt of your writing that shows how you have met each learning outcome. Explain why you selected each piece. Your selection can come from any work you completed, including discussion board entries, reflective writing exercises, freewriting opportunities, and your project drafts.
- Integrating your ideas as a writer with appropriate source material.
  1. Include aspects of your genre analysis or op-ed here.
- Communicating in various rhetorical contexts.
  - Address how each assignment's genre expectations changed the rhetorical choices you made.
- Develop writing projects through multiple drafts (writing, reviewing, revising) as a means to discover and reconsider ideas.
  - Include a section of writing you believe improved over multiple drafts. Provide that same excerpt over three drafts and explain how the writing evolved.

- Experience the collaborative and social aspects of writing through conversations that address the audience and provide productive feedback.
- What feedback was most beneficial from your instructor and classmates?
- Provide an example of a revision that was made from direct feedback from both your instructor and classmate.
- Explain how that revision improved your draft.

SECTION THREE:
STUDENT VOICES

CHAPTER 18

CENTERING THE STUDENT WRITER

Alicia Clark-Barnes and Zac Ginsburg

In this chapter we will look at examples of the assignments described in section 2. In the past, you may have read examples of writing by professional authors to gain inspiration for your writing or to make sure that your approach to an assignment was on the right track. Here we focus on examples written by students completing the same assignments that you are working on. You may wonder if looking at examples of student writing is 'cheating' or if student examples are as valuable as professional ones. In this chapter, we will read rhetorically to explore the resources student examples offer and discuss how to use model essays to strengthen your drafts.

One of the reasons we read student samples is to get a sense of genre conventions. Genre conventions are the stylistic and structural elements that readers come to expect out of a certain type of writing. For example, when we read a narrative, we expect to follow some sort of story arc and experience events through the eyes of a character. Clicking on an online news article, we expect an informative title, an image, a compelling hook, and hyperlinks to sources. The assignments in ENG 110 have genre conventions, too; the literacy narrative, the genre analysis, and the editorial essay are genres that come with certain expectations. Student samples help us understand these expectations.

But what about individuality? What about your own personal voice? Will you lose that if you model your paper off of another student's? The sample student papers are meant to give you a framework. By making yourself aware of what techniques are working well in a sample, you can use what you find helpful to write your paper. For example, you might read a sample literacy narrative that uses a type of story arc that you like. Imagine this author started the story near the end, at the most climactic moment, and then went back to the beginning to tell the whole rest of the story. If this structure hooked your attention, you might try to use that story arc for your own narrative and find that it fits! This is not copying or cheating. This is becoming aware of genre conventions and using them in your own writing.

Another example is reading a sample genre analysis and noticing how the author uses a five-paragraph essay structure with a debatable thesis. Perhaps your own analysis ends up having six paragraphs, but at least you know that three paragraphs would have been too few for this type of assignment. You could also see how the author quoted from and incorporated sources into their paper, including how they formatted in-text citations and the works cited page. Reading sample essays makes us aware of assignment expectations and gives us the framework to write freely without the fear of straying too far from convention.

You might find sources of inspiration in student samples. Maybe you're toying with a topic you think is too personal or too ordinary until you read a sample that turned a seemingly mundane topic into something exciting. You may find you can relate to the experiences of your fellow student writers who sat where you're sitting, have brought their various life experiences into these essays, and are at the same stage of life that you are.

Chapter 18 : Centering the Student Writer

Sure, you don't know these student authors in person the same way you might not know a professional author, but they've chosen to share their papers with you, to help guide you through the unit. It's also important to note that these sample papers aren't perfect, nor are they first drafts. These students worked through a multi-draft process to make improvements each step of the way. What would the next draft have looked like? There's always room to make even a strong paper shine a little brighter.

In the sample literacy narrative, "The Transformative Power of Library Experiences for Children," you may begin your reading by looking at genre conventions. This writer chose to tell a series of short stories focused around one literacy location, the library. As you read through the sample, you may find that you have had similar experiences exploring pop-up or touch-and-feel books. Or you may connect with the writer's sense of wonder and delight, which grows with each return trip.

The writer has organized their narrative chronologically, but you can also notice how the scenes the writer describes gradually increase in complexity. The first scene orients the reader to the children's section then the following scenes bring in sensory detail about the books. These details help the reader distinguish one book from the next and also show the variety of ways the books engage the writer's imagination as she connects with favorite characters and then is challenged to imagine them in new settings, like with Santa on the beach. The story builds to the arts and crafts scene where she replicates an item from the story. Building the teacup causes her to revisit the tea party scenes and engage with a book in a new way.

The writer concludes the narrative by summarizing the impact of the library visits on her personal literacy journey. She then connects her early reading experiences to those of other children. She highlights the role of adults in initiating this journey and brings the story back to the present by reflecting on lifelong learning and the "the endless world of stories waiting to be discovered."

To begin your literacy narrative, list your own literacy experiences and sort through them to select moments that will capture a similar sense of wonder. Or maybe reading the essay reminded you of a specific person who was important to your literacy journey. The writer does not introduce many characters in the library story, but maybe you want to begin, with a scene that includes a dialogue between significant characters. Maybe you did not enjoy reading as a child but will instead tell a more recent story about tackling a challenging writing assignment. You can still return to the sample essay as you draft to revisit how the author transitions from moment to moment or how they introduce a broader takeaway into their conclusion paragraph.

Reading rhetorically and reading student samples are skills writers continue to utilize outside of class as well. Students often turn to model examples when creating resumes. There are many templates for resumes available on the internet. Some templates are designed for people switching careers, while others may be for experienced employees hoping to get a promotion. While it is helpful to look at different types of resumes when designing your own, you will likely find it most helpful to look at a sample done by a student because they will have similar amounts and types of experience to present. You may look at sample resumes to see how much detail is used, how the writer describes tasks, or to understand the types of information the writer chose to include.

As you learn new genres and continue to engage with model texts, you will become more skilled at balancing originality with convention to preserve your voice within each new format.

CHAPTER 19

STUDENT SAMPLE: LITERACY NARRATIVE

Gia Garofalo

The Transformative Power of Library Experiences for Children

My lifelong love for reading and learning took root in the library. These early encounters were not merely just visits to the local library but life-altering experiences that have left a mark on my journey of self-discovery in literature. This essay delves into the profound impact of these childhood library visits, underscoring how they created a want for knowledge and a passion for reading.

My mom brought me to the library one day and I ran straight into the children's section. I was filled with excitement when I came across the pop-up books. Among them, I spotted one of my favorites, "Cinderella." Among them, Cinderella's story came to life in my hands, her golden carriage emerging from the pages shimmering. It was a moment of revelation, a moment when I felt an unbreakable connection to the story itself.

With each weekly visit, more treasures awaited my eager eyes. I explored the shelves when I found another pop-up book. "The Wizard of Oz," I opened it up and out came its three-dimensional tornado. I flipped the pages and next was Emerald City, crafted from iridescent green paper. The pop ups in the book transported me into a world where reality intertwined with fantasy. I marveled at the book's enchanting scenes, drawn into the heart of the story.

Then came the touch and feel books, where the boundaries of the pages seemed to blur. I was so excited when I discovered a book about sea life animals. Sea creatures had always fascinated me as a child, especially dolphins, with their cute and playful nature. I reached out to touch the page, and I felt like I could touch one through the page. I had the rubbery skin of a dolphin touching my hands. As I turned the pages, I could feel the textured scales of fishes and the rough, sandpaper-like skin of a shark. Touch and feel books gave me the wonders of the ocean to life in my hands.

As time passed, at another visit I picked up "Santa's Eleven Months Off," a picture book. The vibrant cover showed Santa Claus lying on a tropical beach, his red suit put over a palm tree. The illustrations within were captivating, each page filled with playful and colorful details. The visual narrative not only enhanced my understanding of the story but also brought out my imagination, making the story more vivid and engaging.

A few weeks went by, and I went to the library again. When I walked in, I saw a group of kids sitting down with an "Alice in Wonderland" sign placed on the table. I found a seat at the table filled with colorful paper, glue, scissors, and markers. As I was thinking if I should take the seat or not, I realized it was a special book-themed craft session. The librarian leading the session told us today's activity was inspired by the story, "Alice in Wonderland." She continued to say we were going to make paper teacups, just like the ones I remembered Alice had in her story. She introduced us to the craft, explaining how it would tie into the book's world. She encouraged us to let our imaginations do the work. I selected vibrant, patterned paper for my teacup. I envisioned a design fit for the Mad

Hatter's tea party. With the scissors in hand, I started cutting out the shapes needed for the cup. As I began assembling the pieces, folding, and gluing them together, it made me think of the scenes in the book where Alice encountered characters and was put into situations. It was like I was creating my own little thing Alice had but right there in the library. Doing the craft made me realize that the book was even more fascinating than I had initially thought. As I finished my paper teacup, I felt a sense of accomplishment. It made me realize the craft deepened my connection to the book. It wasn't just words on a page anymore, it was something from the book I could touch and hold. As I left the library that day, I carried with me not only my paper teacup but also a new love for "Alice in Wonderland."

All these experiences collectively attest to the extraordinary power libraries hold in fostering a passion for reading and encouraging children to seek knowledge independently. For parents and caregivers, the library serves as a gateway to unlocking children's curiosity and kindling their love for learning. The library is a palace of so much exploration, inviting young minds to follow their interests and embark on a personal journey of reading. It empowers children to become lifelong learners, igniting their desire for knowledge and unlocking the endless world of stories waiting to be discovered.

In conclusion, my library adventures were not just visits, they were transformative experiences that shaped my love for books and brought out my curiosity. Through the pages of books and the creative library sessions, I discovered a profound connection with literature. These formative years at the library exemplify its unique role in nurturing young minds, fostering a love for reading, and creating lifelong learners.

CHAPTER 20
STUDENT SAMPLE: GENRE ANALYSIS
Payton Cocchia

Missing White Woman Syndrome: Its Effect

The tragic case of Gabrielle Petito has taken the world by storm. All eyes have been glued to television and smartphone screens anxious to take in more updates involving her disappearance and murder. Many can argue that the attention this young woman and her fiancé have received is solely due to the shocking nature of the case. Others have more than enough reason to believe that this is simply another continual instance of, as the American journalist, Gwen Ifill has referred to it as, "Missing White Woman Syndrome." Within two educational editorials, "The Media Loves Missing White Women" and "The Long American History of 'Missing White Woman Syndrome,'" light is shed onto the dangerous effects of racism and society's prioritization of white women's disappearances over women of color. To further analyze these editorials, using terms such as rhetoric, genre, exigence, and purpose, can act as valuable learning and understanding tools. Rhetoric is simply the act of persuasion, the act of using language and communication to accomplish something. Genre refers to how the subject is presented to the audience, exigence is why the writer is writing, and purpose is what the author is seeking to get from the audience. The communication decisions made, present in both editorials, are very similar. Nevertheless, both writers did choose contrasting structures for their work to get their points across. Julia S. Jordan-Zachery, the writer of the Washington Post article, went about this topic by providing numerous quotes from others who have studied this issue. Helen Rosner, writer of The New Yorker article, instead, chose a question and answer format. Both women expressed and explained the matter very well.

Beginning with Julia S. Jordan-Zachery's piece, "The Media Loves Missing White Women" for *The Washington Post*, this essay focuses on the disturbing lack of media coverage on Black women and their disappearances in comparison to White women, such as Gabby Petito. The main exigence, or reasoning for the rhetoric, is this massive, discriminative, and dangerous issue. The overall fact that Black women's disappearances, abductions, and violent experiences, are going unreported and unnoticed in the mainstream media. This continuous lack of coverage is very dangerous considering that without awareness being spread, missing people(s) remain difficult to locate. "That absence (in media) can best be understood as part of a larger societal attitude toward Black girls and women, in which the American body politic keeps us on the margins of society" ("The Media Loves Missing White Women"). The genre remains informative and educational, similar to a typical editorial. To achieve her main purpose, spreading awareness, Julia included a great amount of research. With added statements and data from law professor Zach Sommers, Harvard Business Review, late journalist Gwen Ifill, as well as other scholars, she was able to supply a lot of valuable information to support the principal idea. "The late journalist, Gwen Ifill is widely considered to have created the concept of missing White woman syndrome, which opened the door for an intersectional analysis of how news media cover missing people"

("The Media Loves Missing White Women"). The structure of this text including vital quotations and data helps create a very organized and enlightening editorial.

Helen Rosner, the writer of "The Long American History of Missing White Woman Syndrome" for *The New Yorker*, takes a fairly different approach when addressing this inequality. Greatly similar to Julia S. Jordan-Zachery, Rosner's piece also shines a light on this syndrome. "The photos of Petito that filled our screens showed an attractive, blond, young white woman who radiated the curated happiness of a social-media native, and critics noted that coverage of her disappearance—and the subsequent identification, in Wyoming, of her remains—dwarfed the attention that both the media and law enforcement pay to other missing and murdered people, especially those who are Black and indigenous" ("The Long American History"). Unlike, Jordan-Zachery's structure, Rosner's article is split up into small sections including her question and true crime scholar and English professor, Jean Murley's answers. "I recently spoke with Murley about the Petito case and its coverage, how news stories are narrativized even as they unfold, and whether a lurid obsession with true crime has any upside. Our conversation has been edited for length and clarity" ("The Long American History"). Throughout these small Q&A segments, many important aspects of Missing White Woman Syndrome are acknowledged.

Both editorials and their contents considered, it is clear that both Julia S. Jordan-Zachery and Helen Rosner are passionate women who are determined in the long-going fight for equality. Regardless of their differing article structures, the same idea is ever present. They share the same exigence, purpose, and genre, but express them uniquely. Anyone who values equal media coverage for all demographics of women, would appreciate their work. In the midst of Gabby Petito's disappearance, countless women of color were missing as well from both their homes and the news. This is not to diminish the horrific death of Gabrielle in any way. However, with constant reports and updates her story received, the same must be done for women and girls of color. Exposing these societal microaggressions that are still happening towards women of color is just another essential step in the fight for justice and building a more inclusive future.

REFERENCES

Jordan-Zachery, J. S. (2021, October 13). Analysis | The media loves 'missing white women.' Black women are already missing from public view. The Washington Post,.https://www.washingtonpost.com/politics/2021/10/14/media-loves-missing-white-women-black-women-are-already-missing-public-view/.

Rosner, H. (2021, October 8). The long American history of 'missing white woman syndrome. The New Yorker. https://www.newyorker.com/news/q-and-a/the-long-american-history-of-missing-white-woman-syndrome.

CHAPTER 21

STUDENT SAMPLE: OPINION EDITORIAL

George Provel

Barry Bonds Belongs in the Hall of Fame

Barry Bonds is the most fearsome hitter to ever step foot in the batter's box in the world. He was capable of doing things that no one has ever done before, and he has all-time records to prove it. The issue was that he was not inducted into the Hall of Fame because he was linked to steroid use, which is a banned substance in Major League Baseball. His career is known to be split into two halves, before steroid use, and after steroid use. Both halves of his career were beyond remarkable due to his strength, speed, power, and overall ability to hit. While some people may disagree that Bonds should be in the Hall of Fame, I feel that he deserves to be in it because he was a very elite hitter who did things that no other player has ever done, and no future players may ever be able to achieve the things he did.

As someone who has played baseball since as I can remember, it was and still is always talked about how great Barry Bonds was. Coaches will frequently use him as an example by explaining something he would do in his swing or have us do drills that he would do. That alone shows how highly he is respected for his talents, and people are unbothered by the fact that he did steroids. Bonds was able to do things that no other player has done and may never do. Before his steroid use, he "had a career batting average of .290 and he had over 400 home runs and stolen bases, the only player to reach that number in both categories" (Wylie). Additionally, he was also a three-time MVP and had 8 Gold Gloves (Wylie). Those statistics alone should be enough to have him in the Hall of Fame, but that only tells the story about half of his career.

After his career was all said and done, he held all-time records in multiple notable categories, and had all around amazing numbers. He has the most home runs in MLB history with 762, has the most walks in history with 2,558, had a career batting average of .298, and had a total of 2,935 hits (Wylie). If someone were to look at these stats and have no idea who the player was, they would say these stats belong to debatably the greatest hitter of all time.

There are hitters who pitchers do not like to face, but then there is Barry Bonds. He instilled a different level of fear into every pitcher every time he stepped up to the plate. He has the all-time records in walks, which speaks volumes showing how pitchers did not want to challenge him. He is also the all-time intentionally walked leader, with 688 (Kline). That means that 688 times, he walked up to the plate and was purposely not even given a chance to hit the ball due to his presence in the batter's box. A great example showing how much pitchers were afraid to challenge Bonds was "in May 1998 he was intentionally walked with the bases loaded in the bottom of the 9th inning, his team trailing by only two" (Wylie). This proves how dominant of a hitter he was because the opposing team was willing to give up a run to potentially lose the game just to not give Bonds the chance to get the game winning hit.

Although critics say Barry Bonds was directly connected to steroid use and that is why he was not inducted into the Hall of Fame, there are people in the Hall of Fame who have also done steroids, or worse things than steroids. Jeff Passan, who is an American Baseball Columnist said that "There already are players in the Hall accused of using PEDs. Or that the commissioner whose tenure encompassed the entirety of the steroid era, Bud Selig, is himself enshrined. Or that generations of players before Bonds, including manifold Hall of Famers, popped amphetamines as part of their pregame routine. Or that others honored with bronze renderings include multiple racists, domestic abusers" (Passan). This shows how truly unfair and unjust it is that he was not inducted because in my books, racists and domestic abusers is by far worse than taking a performance enhancing drug, and even other steroid users are in the Hall as well. To top it off, Bonds is a tremendously better overall player than any of the people that fall into any of those categories. Even though Selig was supposed to monitor and give suspensions to people who were taking steroids if they tested positive, Bonds was never suspended because he never tested positive. This shows that there was leeway given because everybody knew Bonds was connected to steroid use, but since he never actually tested positive, Selig was not going to suspend him due to the amount of money he was bringing into the MLB by more people coming to his games or watching him on television. If there was that much leeway to let players take steroids with no repercussions, then there should be some flexibility in letting Bonds be inducted into the Hall of Fame because he was never punished for doing so.

In conclusion, there are many logical and statistical reasons why Barry Bonds deserves to be in the Hall of Fame. He has numerous extremely impressive all-time records, had a once in a lifetime ability to hit any pitch due to his great hand-eye coordination, freakish strength, and overall, a great athlete. Even though he had so many great statistics, that does not even account for the pure fear his presence gave pitchers when he stepped in the box. Pitchers would try their best to give them their best pitches, or pitch around him, but no matter what they did, it was never enough to contain Bonds's ability to find his way on base or hit the ball out of the park. All these factors play into debatably the greatest hitter that has ever played baseball, yet he does not get the credit he deserves due to doing the same thing many other great players were doing

during his era.

REFERENCES

Kline, A. (2023, April 7). Welcome to baseball analytica. What if pitchers actually pitched to Barry Bonds? Baseball Analytica,. baseball-analytica.com/posts/2023-04-07/if-pitchers-pitched-to-bonds.

Passan, J. (2022, January 25). If Barry Bonds isn't a hall of famer by the end of the day, it's a failure by the Hall of Fame. ESPN.com. www.espn.com/mlb/story/_/id/33138884/if-barrybonds-hall-famer-end-day-failure-hall-fame.

Wylie, C. (2019, February 5). Opinion: Barry Bonds should belong in the Hall of Fame. The Liberty Champion.www.liberty.edu/champion/2019/02/opinion-barry-bondsshould-belong-in-the-halloffame/#:~:text=With%20only%20three%20years%20of%20voting%20eligibility%20remaining%2C,Bonds%20absolutely%20belongs%20in%20the%20Hall%20of%20Fame.

STUDENT SAMPLE: OPINION EDITORIAL
Victoria DiCecco

Powerless After the Storm: Puerto Rios's Endless Struggle

Since I can remember, my family has flown to Puerto Rico every year to visit my grandparents and family on the island. When we are not there, we make it a point to speak to them on the phone multiple times a week. When Hurricane Maria struck the island in 2017, we lost all contact with them for months. We went through every day wondering if they were safe, if their homes were okay, and when we would hear their voices again. When we finally got a call from them, it was short. It was just enough to hear my grandfather say, "We are okay, and the house is okay," before the call got disconnected. We were able to visit them the following two summers, in 2018 and 2019 before COVID shut everything down. Then in September 2022, Hurricane Fiona hit the island. Though it was not as bad as Hurricane Maria, the island once again was left struggling. Luckily, we were able to visit in April of 2023. As we drove from the airport to my grandparent's home, I saw the fallen trees and broken roads, and a small broken down bridge that went over a creek. People were repairing it as we passed by, but I was told that the damage to that bridge had been done during Hurricane Maria, not Hurricane Fiona. That means that even seven years later, the bridge had still not been fixed.

From August to September, Puerto Ricans are faced with many struggles as this is peak hurricane season for the island. The media tends to only share stories from major storms. Hurricane Fiona and Hurricane Maria may be the first to come to some people's minds when discussing this topic. In reality, these storms hit the island every year, making it difficult for recovery around the island. With these annual disasters, the island should have a strong government and reliable systems to help them get back on their feet. However, it has been shown time and time again that the people of Puerto Rico are often left helpless. Puerto Rico's electrical system, LUMA plays a big role in this support as many are left without power for long periods. My grandparents, for example, had no power for nine months after Maria. When the higher authorities are not meeting the demands of the islands and the people's needs, it leaves the people to have to take matters into their own hands. It is an overwhelming cycle for citizens as these hurricanes are unavoidable, and they are left to take care of their homes and towns as a community. Awareness needs to be raised amongst people within the island, and also from outside sources to make a change in the island's way of dealing with natural disasters.

To begin, some argue that Puerto Rico's government has improved and is doing what they can to help their people. However, after analyzing the situation, and looking at it from different perspectives, this is proven to be incorrect. For example, "But there is reason for hope. While Puerto Rico's Department of Justice, which is responsible for the enforcement of the local law, allows impunity to go unchecked, Washington has begun to pay attention" (Ayala, par.10). This shows that outsiders are becoming involved in the situation. Ayala goes on to explain that the former governor and past governors were being charged and accused of corruption. However, people shouldn't have to rely on others to make changes in their local government. Additionally, there's only so much that outside sources can do. While the awareness is beneficial, change needs to be made within Puerto Rico's local government.

After the storm season, devastation is seen across the whole island. Even years following Hurricane Maria, one of the major storms that left many residents hopeless, devastation across the land can still be seen. For example, "Its powerful winds, with gusts exceeding 100 m.p.h., destroyed thousands of homes and wiped out the island's agriculture and access to communications" (Sánchez and Mazzei, par. 21). This shows the impact of Hurricane Maria. Of course, you cannot blame anyone for these circumstances. Puerto Ricans know of the possibilities that come with owning a home and land on the island. However, what makes this situation so concerning is how authorities go about helping their people. "Recovery was painfully sluggish, and the lack of potable water, fuel, and food supplies in the wake of the storm prompted an exodus of tens of thousands of residents to the United States mainland" (Sánchez and Mazzei, par. 21). Due to LUMA's poor leadership and planning, people were forced to leave their homes. As mentioned, people know the hardships they might face during storm season. If they know it, then the government should know it as well. They should be prepared for worst case scenarios following storms, in order to quickly care for their people and help everyone get back on their feet. Instead, people have to wait and live in these harsh conditions, well past the time that they should be. Even those fortunate enough to leave, shouldn't have to leave because of the failures made by the government.

The slow recovery after storms raises more concerns than just economic and environmental stress. Homes, buildings, and schools were destroyed after Hurricane Maria. Students were not able to return to school after the storm. If there was a chance the building was still standing, it was likely to not even have power. With Hurricane Maria coming in September, students missed a big chunk of the start of their school year. Moriah Balingit, in "In Puerto Rico, Living and Learning in the Dark as Schools Struggle to Recover from Hurricane Maria," expresses many of the struggles students faced following the storm. She tells the story of a specific family to show one of many situations. In this case, "Julio did not return to class until late October, and Neida in mid-November. They were lucky. In other parts of the island, children did not return until December, missing nearly three months" (Balingit, par. 3). To miss this amount of school plays a big role on a child. At a young age, education is so important, and attending school greatly impacts a child's development. We saw this during the Covid lockdown in 2020, and the way that children were affected by not being in school. Since LUMA could not get to every family's home, some were left without power for over a year. The difference between this situation and COVID-19 is that during COVID-19, students were still able to get some level of education through electronic devices. However, without power after the storms, this could not be accomplished. Furthermore, Balingit also addresses how over 25,000 students were forced to leave the island and move to the States to continue their education. Many of them had to leave without their families. If the government and LUMA had planned better, and done more to enhance recovery, children could have attended school while staying with their families, which should have been a given.

Clearly, many reasons support why the government and LUMA need to do better for the residents. Homes are destroyed, people don't have access to basic amenities, they can't contact their families and students cannot go to school. These are just a few of the hardships the people face on top of the stress of enduring the storm. If these authorities continue to fail Puerto Ricans, the community of the island will start to diminish. There is already a distrust that the residents have built since Hurricane Maria. After seeing the damage the storm did, and the lack of support they received, they feel like they are on their own. Children were forced to leave their families to attend school, and people left their homes after receiving no help. People will continue to leave, and the island's quality will decrease. What was once a beautiful island, will become rundown and uncared for.

Hurricane season is part of the deal when you decide to live in Puerto Rico. Storms are inevitable, and many people learn how to prepare for them. While LUMA, the government, and other authorities do try to take a step in helping the island with recovery, it is still not enough. It is imperative that outside sources step in and provide the help that Puerto Rico needs to maintain the quality of the island. If authorities continue to neglect the people's and island's needs, it will eventually diminish the community and create a bad environment. As these authorities have repeatedly failed to do the right thing for the people, they are left to look to external sources for support. More people need to learn about these issues to raise awareness and help Puerto Rico's authorities take a step in the right direction.

REFERENCES

Ayala, I. M. (2022, September, 23). Betrayal and blackouts in Puerto Rico. New York Times.link.gale.com/apps/doc/A719044496/GBIB?u=nysl_me_pace&sid=bookmark-GBIB&xid=2a8bce04. Accessed 7 Dec. 2023.

Balingit, M. (2018, January 29). In Puerto Rico, living and learning in the dark as schools struggle to recover from Hurricane Maria. Washington Post. link.gale.com/apps/doc/A525477161/GBIB?u=nysl_me_pace&sid=bookmark-GBIB&xid=f5f9422c. Accessed 7 Dec. 2023.

Pérez Sánchez, L. N. & Patricia M. (2022, September 19). On anniversary of Hurricane Maria, storm Leaves Puerto Rico in the dark. The New York Times. www.nytimes.com/2022/09/19/us/puerto-rico-power-hurricane-fiona.html?smid=url-share.

Editor and Contributor Bios

Robert Mundy

Dr. Robert Mundy is an Associate Professor in the Department of English, Writing, and Cultural Studies, where he serves as Chair and Director of Composition. His teaching and research focus on theories of composition and rhetoric, writing program administration and assessment, and gender and masculinity studies. He is the author of *Gender, Sexuality and the Cultural Politics of Men's Identity in the New Millennium and Out in the Center: Public Controversies, Private Struggles*, winner of the 2019 International Writing Center Association Book Award.

Alysa Robin Hantgan

Alysa is Associate Chair and lecturer in the Department of English, Writing, and Cultural Studies at Pace University. She holds an M.F.A. in Fiction from Sarah Lawrence College and a B.A. in Communication from the University of Michigan. She is the Chair of the Affordable Learning Initiative and has a special interest in the availability of high-quality and affordable learning materials. Her writing and research can be read in Post Road, The Forum, Journal of Multimodal Rhetorics, and elsewhere.

Justine Matias

Justine Matias is a dedicated adjunct professor with a passion for language and literacy. She has taught composition and rhetoric since 2020 and specializes in first-year composition pedagogy.

Christina Gonzalez

Christina (Tina) Gonzalez is a LatinX educator, writer, and scholar who teaches English, Women's and Gender Studies, and Composition in New York and New Jersey. Her scholarly research and pedagogical interests include Labor-Based Grading, Open Education Resources, and Anti-Racist Education. Her pedagogy focuses on equitability, social justice, and transcendence to empower communities that have long been silenced and oppressed. She is a graduate of NYU (BA) and Sarah Lawrence (MFA).

Katherine Dye

Katherine Dye is a fiction writer and an adjunct professor of writing at Pace University. She has been teaching writing and composition since 2022 and holds an M.F.A. in Writing from Sarah Lawrence College and a B.A. in Comparative Literature from Oberlin College.

Jack N. Morales

Jack N. Morales is an Assistant Professor of Writing and Cultural Studies at Pace University, where he studies rhetorical education and its impact on the history of higher education. His current project, The People's College: Race, Rhetoric, and Higher Education Reform 1964-1981, is a rhetorical history of the U.S. community college during the post-Civil Rights Era. When he is not teaching or doing research, Dr. Morales enjoys bowling, swimming, and training for long-distance races.

Editor and Contributor Bios

Genevieve Mills
Genevieve Mills is an adjunct English professor. She has a Bachelor's in English and French from the University of Louisville and an MFA in Creative Writing with a concentration in Speculative Fiction from Sarah Lawrence College. She also teaches English as a Second Language.

Zac Ginsburg
Zac Ginsburg is a creative writer and member of the adjunct faculty at Pace University, where he also works as a tutor in the Learning Commons. He holds an M.F.A. in Fiction from The New School and a B.A. in English from Wesleyan University. His writing has appeared in Wired, The Brooklyn Rail, The Adroit Journal, and elsewhere.

Erika J. Pichardo
Erika J. Pichardo is an adjunct professor in Writing and Cultural Studies at the Pleasantville campus for Pace University. She has taught ENG 201 Writing in the Disciplines for five years and specializes in labor-based grading to best support students in their academic writing. She holds a Ph.D. in criminal justice with a specialization in law and public policy.

Alicia Clark-Barnes
Alicia Clark-Barnes is an adjunct professor in Writing and Cultural Studies and the manager of writing support for the Learning Commons at Pace University, Pleasantville. She holds a PhD in rhetoric and composition from the University of New Hampshire.

Dana Jaye Cadman
Dana Jaye Cadman is an Assistant Professor and Director of Creative Writing for Pace University Pleasantville and holds an MFA from Rutgers-Newark. Her poetry has appeared in New England Review, PRISM International, Southeast Review, Academy of American Poets' Poem-A-Day, and elsewhere. Find her on danajaye.com

Jessica Kiebler
As an Instruction Librarian, Jessica Kiebler educates students and faculty about the research process and the library. Her expertise in information literacy provides a backdrop for her work in source type and genre exploration. She enjoys working with English faculty to engage students with research through writing education.

Shirli Sela-Levavi
Shirli Sela-Levavi earned her Ph.D. in Comparative Literature from Rutgers, New Brunswick. Her scholarly work focuses on Hebrew and Jewish literature. She works as an editor and translator at Resling Publishing House, Israel, and teaches first-year writing and rhetoric at Pace University and NJIT.

References

Alexander, K. P. (2023). Reconceptualizing literacy: Experimentation and play in audio literacy narratives. Computers and Composition, 69, 102790–102790. https://doi.org/10.1016/j.compcom.2023.102790

American Library Association. (2024). Information literacy. https://literacy.ala.org/information-literacy/

Aristotle. (1994-1998). Rhetoric. (W. Rhys Roberts,Trans.)https://www.bocc.ubi.pt/pag/Aristotle-rhetoric.pdf

Ayala, I. M. (2022, September, 23). Betrayal and blackouts in Puerto Rico. New York Times.link.gale.com/apps/doc/A719044496/GBIB?u=nysl_me_pace&sid=bookmark-GBIB&xid=2a8bce04. Accessed 7 Dec. 2023.

Baker-Bell, A. (2020). Linguistic justice: Black language, literacy, identity, and pedagogy. Routledge & National Council of Teachers of English.

Balingit, M. (2018, January 29). In Puerto Rico, living and learning in the dark as schools struggle to recover from Hurricane Maria. Washington Post. link.gale.com/apps/doc/A525477161/GBIB?u=nysl_me_pace&sid=bookmark-GBIB&xid=f5f9422c. Accessed 7 Dec. 2023.

Barila, B. (2016). Integrating mindfulness into anti-oppression pedagogy. Routledge.

Bartholomae, D. (1986). Inventing the university. Journal of Basic Writing, 5(1), 4-23. https://doi.org/10.37514/JBW-J.1986.5.1.02

Bawarshi, A., & Reiff, M. J. (2010). Genre: An introduction to history, theory, research, and pedagogy. https://openlibrary.org/books/OL24099291M/Genre

Bazerman, C. (2010). The informed writer: Using sources in the disciplines. The WAC Clearinghouse. https://wac.colostate.edu/books/practice/informedwriter/

Bazerman, C. (2013). A Rhetoric of Literate Action: Literate Action Volume 1. WAC Clearinghouse. https://doi.org/10.37514/PER-B.2013.0513

Bitzer, L.F. (1968). The Rhetorical Situation. Philosophy and Rhetoric. 1 (1), pp. 1-14. https://www.jstor.org/stable/40236733

Bizzell, P. (1992). Academic Discourse and Critical Consciousness. University of Pittsburgh Press.

Bizzell, P. (2003). Cognition, convention, and certainty: what we need to know about writing. In Victor Villanueva (Ed.), Cross talk in comp theory: a reader (pp. 387-412). NCTE.

Bratta, P. and Powell, M. (2016, April 20). Introduction to the Special Issue: Entering the Cultural Rhetorics Conversations. Enculturation: A Journal of Rhetoric, Writing, and Culture. https://enculturation.net/entering-the-cultural-rhetorics-conversations

Braziller, A., & Kleinfeld, E. (2020). The Bedford book of genres: A guide and reader. Bedford Books.

Bryson, K. (2012). The Literacy Myth in the Digital Archive of Literacy Narratives. Computers and Composition, 29(3), 254–268. https://doi.org/10.1016/j.compcom.2012.06.001

Burnell, C., Wood, J., Babin, M., Pesznecker, S., & Rosevear, N. (2020). The word on college reading and writing. Center for Open Education University of Minnesota. https://openoregon.pressbooks.pub/wrd/

The Carnegie Foundation for the Advancement of Teaching. (2007). The Carnegie Unit: What is it? The State University of New York. https://system.suny.edu/media/suny/content-assets/documents/faculty-senate/ugrad/TheCarnegieUnit.pdf

Carter, M. (2007). Ways of knowing, doing, and writing in the disciplines. College Composition and Communication, 58(3), 385–418. http://www.jstor.org/stable/20456952

Clark, I. L., & Hernandez, A. (2011). Genre awareness, academic argument, and transferability. The WAC Journal, 22(1), 65–78. https://doi.org/10.37514/wac-j.2011.22.1.05

Cobain, K. (1991). Come as you are [Song]. On Nevermind [Album]. DGC Records.

Covert, B. (2021, July 20). 8 hours a day, 5 days a week is not working for Us. New York Times. https://www.nytimes.com/2021/07/20/opinion/covid-return-to-office.html

Crank, V. (2012). From high school to college: Developing writing skills in the disciplines. The WAC Journal, 23(1), 49–63. https://doi.org/10.37514/wac-j.2012.23.1.04

References 149

Cronkhite, T. (n.d.) 7. Kairos. Rhetorical Choices. Aims Community College.https://pressbooks.pub/words/chapter/chapter-7-kairos/

DeJoy, N. (2004). Undergraduate writing in composition studies. Utah State University Press.

Dempsey, J. (2023, January 18). AI: Arguing its Place in Higher Education. Higher Education Digest. https://www.highereducationdigest.com/ai-arguing-its-place-in-higher-education/

DePeter, R. (2020). How to Write Meaningful Peer Response Praise. In D.L. Driscoll, M. Stewart & M. Vetter(Eds.), Writing Spaces: Readings on Writing Vol. 3) (pp. 40-51). Parlor Press. https://writingspaces.org/past-volumes/how-to-write-meaningful-peer-response-prais/

Devitt, A.J., Reiff, M.J., & Bawarshi, A. (2004). Scenes of writing: strategies for composing with genres. Pearson/Longman.

Devitt, A. J. (2009). Teaching critical genre awareness. In The WAC Clearinghouse; Parlor Press eBooks, 341–354. https://doi.org/10.37514/per-b.2009.2324.2.17

Duffy, W. (2023). What is Rhetoric? A "Choose Your Own Adventure" Primer. (T. Daniels-Lerberg, D. Driscoll, M.K. Stewart, M. Vetter, Ed.) Writing Spaces: Readings on Writing, Volume 5 (pp. 247-265) WAC Clearinghouse. https://wac.colostate.edu/docs/books/writingspaces5/15Duffy.pdf

Dweck, C. S. (2016). Mindset: The new psychology of success. Ballantine Books.

Elbow, P. (1998). Writing without teachers. Oxford University Press.

Elbow, P. (1995). Being a writer vs. being an academic: A conflict of goals. College Composition and Communication, 46(1), 72-83. https://doi.org/10.2307/358871

Elbow, P. (1998). Writing with power. Oxford University Press.

Fluckiger, J. (2010). Single Point Rubric: A Tool for Responsible Student Self-Assessment.Teacher Education Faculty Publications, 5. https://digitalcommons.unomaha.edu/tedfacpub/5

Ford Motor Company. (2022). 2022 Ford escape owner's manual. Ford Motor Co. https://www.fordservicecontent.com/Ford_Content/vdirsnet/OwnerManual/Home/

Freire, P. (2000). Pedagogy of the oppressed (M.B. Ramos, Trans.) Continuum. (Original work published 1968)

Gagich, M. and Zickel, E. (n.d.). 6.4 Rhetorical Appeals: Logos, Pathos, and Ethos Defined. A Guideto Rhetoric, Genre, and Success in First-Year Writing. MSL Academic Endeavors.https://pressbooks.ulib.csuohio.edu/csu-fyw-rhetoric/chapter/rhetorical-strategies-buildng-compelling-arguments/

Gagich, M., & Zickel, E. (2018). A guide to rhetoric, genre, and success in first-year writing. MSL Academic Endeavors Imprint of Michael Schwartz Library at Cleveland State University. https://pressbooks.ulib.csuohio.edu/csu-fyw-rhetoric/

Gardner, T. (n.d.). When your grades are based on labor. https://tracigardner.com/labor/

Gee, J. P. (1989). What is literacy? Journal of Education, 171(1), pp. 18-23.

Gee, J. P. (1990). Social linguistics and literacies: Ideology in discourses. London: Falmer Press.

Getchall, K. & Gonso, K. (2019). Valuing the process: Building a foundation for collaborative peer review. Teaching English in the Two-Year College, 47(1), 63–75. https://doi.org/10.58680/tetyc201930324

Giles, S. L. (2010). Reflective writing and the revision process: What were you thinking? In C. Lowe & P. Zemliansky (Eds.), Writing Spaces: Readings on Writing (pp. 191–204). Parlor Press.

https://writingspaces.org/past-volumes/reflective-writing-and-the-revision-process-what-were-you-thinking/Gillespie, P. & Lerner, N. (2008). The longman guide to peer tutoring (2nd ed.). Pearson Longman.

Gilyard, K. (1991). Voices of the self: A study of language competence. Wayne State University Press.

Grauman, J. (2002). What's that supposed to mean? Using feedback on your writing. InD.Driscoll, M. Heise, M. Stewart & M. Vetter (Eds.), Writing spaces: Reading on writing (Vol. 4)(pp. 145-165). Parlor Press.

Hall, S. (1997). Introduction, In S. Hall (Ed.), Representation: Cultural Representations and Signifying Practices (pp. 1-11). SAGE Publications.

Hanish, C. (1970). The personal is political. In S. Firestone & A. Koedt (Eds.), Notes from the second year: Women's liberation (pp. 76-77). Radical Feminism.

Hantgan, A. R., & Mundy, R. (2024, August 5). Beyond the single classroom: A model for program-wide alternative grading. Beyond the Single Classroom: A Model for Program-Wide Alternative Grading. https://gradingforgrowth.com/p/beyond-the-single-classroom-a-model

Harris, J. (1989). The idea of community in the study of writing. College Composition and Communication, 40(1), 11-22. https://doi.org/10.2307/358177

hooks, b. (1994). Teaching to transgress: Education as the practice of freedom. Routledge.

Horning, A.S. & Kraemer, E.W. (2013). Reconnecting reading and writing: Introduction and overview. In A. S. Horning & E. W. Kraemer (Eds.), Reconnecting reading and writing (pp. 5-25). Parlor Press Parlor Press; The WAC Clearinghouse. https://wac.colostate.edu/books/referenceguides/reconnecting/

IBM. (2024). What is artificial intelligence (AI).https://www.ibm.com/topics/artificial-intelligence

Inman, J. O. & Powell, R. A. (2018). In the absence of grades. Conference on College Composition and Communication, 7(1), 30-56.https://www.jstor.org/stable/10.2307/26772544

Inoue, A. B. (2022). Labor-Based Grading Contracts: Building Equity and Inclusion in the Compassionate Writing Classroom, 2nd ed. The WAC Clearinghouse; University Press of Colorado. https://doi.org/10.37514/PER-B.2022.1824

Inoue, A. B. (2023). Labor-based grading contracts: Building Equity and inclusion in the compassionate classroom. WAC Clearinghouse.

Jacobson, B., Pawlowski, M., & Tardy, C. (2021). Make your "move": Writing in genres. In C. Lowe & P. Zemliansky (Eds.), Writing Spaces: Readings on Writing (217-238). Parlor Press.

Jordan-Zachery, J. S. (2021, October 13). Analysis | The media loves 'missing white women.' Black women are already missing from public view. The Washington Post,.https://www.washingtonpost.com/politics/2021/10/14/media-loves-missing-white-women-black-women-are-already-missing-public-view/.

Kansas University. (n.d.). Using AI Ethically in Writing Assignments. https://cte.ku.edu/ethical-use-ai-writing-assignments

Kelly, E. E. (2003). The good, the bad, and the ugly of peer review. In T. Daniels-Lerberg, D.L.Driscoll, M. Stewart & M. A. Vetter (Eds.). Writing spaces: Reading on writing (Vol. 5)(pp. 299-317). Parlor Press.

King, M. L, Jr. (2010). I Have a Dream [speech transcript]. NPR. https://www.npr.org/2010/01/18/122701268/i-have-a-dream-speech-in-its-entirety.

Kline, A. (2023, April 7). Welcome to baseball analytica. What if pitchers actually pitched to Barry Bonds? Baseball Analytica,. baseball-analytica.com/posts/2023-04-07/if-pitchers-pitched-to-bonds.

Kohn, A. (2011). The case against grades. Educational Leadership, 69(3), pp. 28-33/ https://www.alfiekohn.org/article/case-grades/

Kohn, A. (2020). Forward. In S. D. Blum (1st Edition), Ungrading (pp. xxii-xix). West Virginia University Press.

Kryger, K. & Zimmerman, G. X. neurodivergence and intersectionality in labor-based grading contracts. Journal of Writing Assessment, 12(2), https://escholarship.org/uc/item/0934x4

Kynard, C. (2007). "I want to be African": In search of a Black radical tradition/African-American-vernacularized paradigm for "Students' right to their own language," critical literacy, and "class politics." College English, 69(4), 360–90.

Lacy, S., & Gagich, E. (2017). The Writing Process, Composing, and Revising. A Guide to Rhetoric, Genre, and Success in First-Year Writing. Pressbooks.

Lamott, A. (2005). Shitty first drafts. In P. Eschholz, A. Rosa, & V. Clark (Eds.), Language awareness: Readings for college writers (pp. 93-96). Boston: Bedford/St. Martin.

Lopate. P. (2013). To Show and To Tell: The Craft of Literary Nonfiction. Free Press.

Lyiscott, J. (2019). Black appetite. White food: Issues of race, voice, and justice within and beyond the classroom. Routledge

Manivannan, V. (n.d.). Statement on AI and Writing. Pace University Writing-Enhanced Course Program Guidebook. chrome-extension://efaidnbmnnnibpcajpcglclefindmkaj/https://www.pace.edu/sites/default/files/2023-09/dyson-writing-enhanced-courses-guidebook.pdf

Martinez, A. Y. (2022). Counterstory: The rhetoric and writing of critical race theory. Conference on College Composition and Communication, National Council of Teachers of English.

Matsuda, P. E. (2006). The myth of linguistic homogeneity in U.S. college composition. College English,

References

68(6), 637-651. https://doi.org/10.2307/25472180

McNulty, B. (2021). The Ability of Identity: An Ever-Changing Word, In A. Von Berg (Ed.), Rhetoricin Everyday Life. Library Partners Press.https://librarypartnerspress.pressbooks.pub/rhetoricineverydaylife/chapter/the-ability-of-identity-an-ever-changing-word-by-braxton-mcnulty/#:~:text=While%20somebody%27s%20personal%20definition%20of,relationships%20are%20formed%20in%20society

Miller, C. L. (1984). Genre as social action. Quarterly Journal of speech, 70(2), 151–167. https://doi.org/10.1080/00335638409383686

Miller, C. R. (1984). Genre as social action. Quarterly Journal of Speech, 70(2), 151–167.

Murray, D. (1984). Write to learn. Harcourt College Publishers.

Murray, D. M. (2024). Teach Writing as a Process Not Product. In K.L. Arola & V. Villanueva (Eds). Cross-talk in comp theory. NCTE.

Nilson, L. (2015). Specific grading: Restoring rigor, motivating students, and saving faculty time. Routledge.

Northwestern University. (2023, November 30). Using AI tools in your research. https://libguides.northwestern.edu/ai-tools-research/acad-integ

Pace University. (2017, September 1). Pace University academic integrity code. https://www.pace.edu/sites/default/files/files/student-handbook/pace-university-academic-integrity-code.pdf

Passan, J. (2022, January 25). If Barry Bonds isn't a hall of famer by the end of the day, it's a failure by the Hall of Fame. ESPN.com. www.espn.com/mlb/story/_/id/33138884/if-barrybonds-hall-famer-end-day-failure-hall-fame.

Pérez Sánchez, L. N. & Patricia M. (2022, September 19). On anniversary of Hurricane Maria, storm Leaves Puerto Rico in the dark. The New York Times. www.nytimes.com/2022/09/19/us/puerto-rico-power-hurricane-fiona.html?smid=url-share.

Perl, S. (1979). The composing processes of unskilled college writers. Research in the Teaching of English, 13(4), 317-336. https://www.jstor.org/stable/40170774

"Popular and Commercial Culture." (2018, June 7) National Park Service. https://www.nps.gov/stli/learn/historyculture/statue-adn-popular-culture.htm

Porter, J. E. (1986). Intertextuality and the discourse community. Rhetoric Review, 5(1), pp. 34-47.

Pratt, M. L. (1999). Ways of Reading (5th edition). In D. Bartholomae & A. Petroksky (Eds). Arts of the contact zone.New York: Bedford/St. Martin's.

Purdue Owl. (2024). Evaluating sources: Where to begin. Purdue University. https://owl.purdue.edu/owl/research_and_citation/conducting_research/evaluating_sources_of_information/where_to_begin.html

Rider, J. (1991). Must imitation be the mother of invention? Journal of Teaching Writing, 9(2), 175-185.

Rodríguez, R. J. (2017). Leave yourself out of your writing. In C.E. Ball & D.M. Loewe (Eds). Bad ideas about writing (pp. 131-133).

Rosner, H. (2021, October 8). The long American history of 'missing white woman syndrome. The New Yorker. https://www.newyorker.com/news/q-and-a/the-long-american-history-of-missing-white-woman-syndrome.

Sackett & Wilhelms Corp, N.Y. (1917). American WWI Poster: Remember Your First Thrill of AMERICAN LIBERTY OUR DUTY - But United States Government Bonds 2nd Liberty Loan of 1917 [Advertisement]. Retrieved May 5, 2024, from https://commons.wikipedia.org/wiki/File:Novum_Eboracum.jpg.

Seow, A. (2002). The Writing Process and Process Writing. In J. C. Richards & W. A. Renandya (Eds.), Methodology in Language Teaching: An Anthology of Current Practice (pp. 315–320). Cambridge: Cambridge University Press.

Skomski, K. (2013). first-year writers: Forward movement, backward progress. In A. S. Horning & E. W. Kraemer (Eds.), Reconnecting reading and writing (pp. 89-107). Parlor Press Parlor Press; The WAC Clearinghouse.https://wac.colostate.edu/books/referenceguides/reconnecting/

Smitherman, G. (1996). Talkin and testifyin: The Language of Black America. Wayne State University. Press.

Sommers, N., & Saltz, L. (2004). The novice as expert: Writing the freshman year. College Composition and Communication, 56(1), 124-149. https://doi.org/10.2307/4140684

Straub, R. (1999). Responding–really responding–to other students' writing. In W. Bishop (Ed.), the Subject is Writing, (2nd ed.) (pp. 136-146). Boynton/Cook Publishers.

Students' right to their own language (1974). Conference on College Composition and Communication. https://cccc.ncte.org/cccc/resources/positions/srtolsummary

Sutch, R. (2015, December 4). Liberty Bonds. Federal Reserve History. https://www.federalreservehistory.org/essays/liberty-bonds

Swales, J. M. (1990). Genre analysis: English in academic and research settings. Cambridge UP.

Swales, J. M. (2017). The concept of discourse community: some recent personal history. Composition Forum, 37. https://compositionforum.com/issue/37/swales-retrospective.php

Teaching & Learning, University Libraries. (2015). Choosing & using sources: A guide to academic research. The Ohio State University. https://ohiostate.pressbooks.pub/choosingsources/

Tonouchi, L. A. (2004). Da state of pidgin address. College English, 67(1), 75-82. https://doi.org/10.2307/4140726

United States Department of Education. (2011. May 18). Guidance to institutions and accrediting agencies regarding a credit hour as defined in the final regulations published on October 29, 2010. Department of Education. https://fsapartners.ed.gov/sites/default/files/attachments/dpcletters/GEN1106.pdf

The University of Arizona. (2023). What is academic integrity, and how can I achieve it? University of Arizona Global Campus. https://www.uagc.edu/blog/what-is-academic-integrity-and-how-can-i-achieve-it#:~:text=your%20college%20assignments.-,What%20is%20Academic%20Integrity%3F,contribute%20to%20the%20academic%20conversation.%E2%80%9D

University of Illinois-Champaign. (2024, October 24). AI in Schools: Pros and Cons. https://education.illinois.edu/about/news-events/news/article/2024/10/24/ai-in-schools--pros-and-cons

Wang, Z. (2022). Computer-assisted EFL writing and evaluations based on artificial intelligence: a case from a college reading and writing course. Library Hi Tech, 40(1), 80–97. https://doi.org/10.1108/LHT-05-2020-0113

The Writing Center. (2024). Academic integrity. University of North Carolina at Chapel Hill. https://writingcenter.unc.edu/esl/resources/academic-integrity/

Wylie, C. (2019, February 5). Opinion: Barry Bonds should belong in the Hall of Fame. The Liberty Champion.www.liberty.edu/champion/2019/02/opinion-barry-bondsshould-belong-in-the-hall of fame/#:~:text=With%20only%20three%20years%20of%20voting%20eligibility%20remaining%2C,Bonds%20absolutely%20belongs%20in%20the%20Hall%20of%20Fame.

Yood, J. (2005). Present-process: The composition of change. Journal of Basic Writing, 24(2),4–25. https://doi.org/10.37514/jbw-j.2005.24.2.02

Young, V. A. Should writers use they own English? Iowa Journal of Cultural Studies, 12(1), 110-117. https://doi.org/10.17077/2168-569X.1095

Young, V. A., Barrett, R., Young-Rivera, Y., & Lovejoy, K. B. (2014). Other people's English: Code-meshing, code-switching, and African American literacy. Teachers College Press.

Scan the QR code to access supplemental materials in the digital companion that support and expand on this text.

The first volume of *Come As You Are*
was published in August 2025
by Pace University Press

Editors: Alysa Robin Hantgan and Robert Mundy

Cover and interior layout by Kayleigh Woltal
The journal was typeset in Garamond Premier Pro and Tenso
and printed by Lightning Source in La Vergne, Tennessee

Pace University Press

Director: Manuela Soares
Faculty Advisor: Eileen Kreit
Production Consultant: Joseph Caserto

Graduate Assistants: Vidhi Sampat and Zetta Whiting
Student Aide: Kianna Swingle and Oriana Galvis-Marvin

www.ingramcontent.com/pod-product-compliance
Lightning Source LLC
Chambersburg PA
CBHW060822190426
43197CB00038B/2197